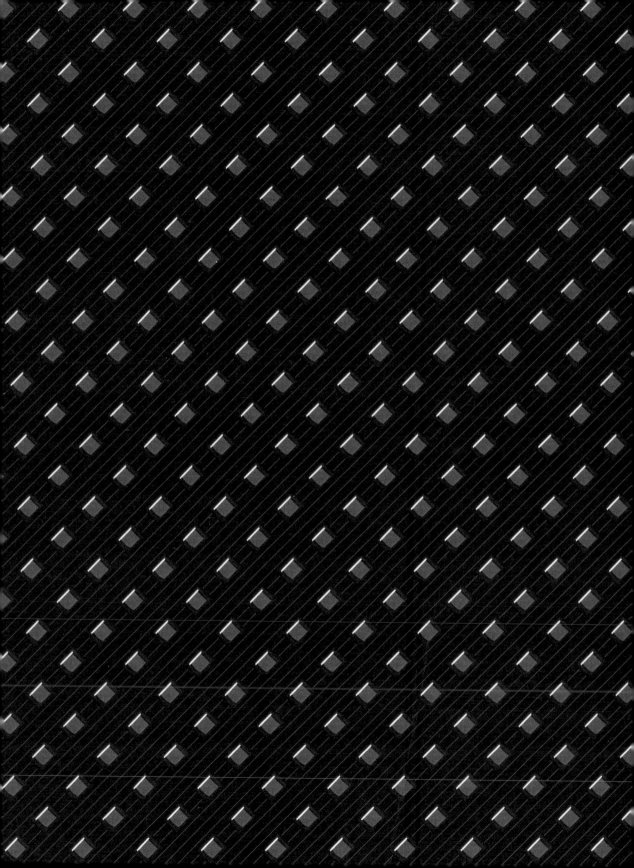

I'M JUST HERE
FOR THE DRINKS

A guide to spirits, drinking and more than 100 extraordinary cocktails

SOTHER TEAGUE
PHOTOGRAPHS BY ERIC MEDSKER

MEDIA LAB BOOKS ·
NEW YORK

Table of Contents

Even in a profession brimming with people boasting fiction-worthy handles (Ivy Mix, Jackson Cannon, Todd Thrasher, Marco Dionysos, Del Pedro, Thad Vogler, St. John Frizell—these are all real bartenders), Sother's stood out. The second thing I noticed about him was his 90-Day Sour, which he served when he worked at a bar called Rye in Brooklyn. Though 2009 was a heady year for modern mixology, a sour that was aged like a wine or a cheese still stood out.

I learned soon enough that there were many remarkable things about Sother that set him apart from the drink-slingin' crowd. His winter-ready United States Postal Service hat, which he wears during shifts and calls his "oldest and most prized possession"; his time with Food Network's *Good Eats*, where he worked as research chef; the size of his East Village bar, Amor y Amargo, which may be the smallest successful watering hole in the United States; his encyclopedic knowledge of bitters, both the kind you dash into cocktails and the kind you sip straight; and his eschewing of citrus in his Amor y Amargo mixing, that 90-Day Sour notwithstanding.

Amor y Amargo is one of a handful of New York cocktail bars I recommend to people unreservedly. It's not so much that the drinks are good (they are, reliably) or that the space is inviting (cozy is the word) or that the crowd is appealing (a bitters bar does not attract louts). It's that Sother is often there. In a bar world increasingly plagued by globe-trotting, absentee bartenders, Sother is unusually dedicated to his small corner of the world. That, to me, is the truest indicator of a passionate bartender, that he simply be there for his customers.

Sit at one of Amor y Amargo's few stools long enough and you're bound to learn a thing or two. With its stock of bitters, books and barware, the bar is as much a school as a saloon, with Sother as its dean and sole instructor. The man talks fast and tirelessly; you can't help but pick up some knowledge and an opinion or two between first order and settling up. A good bit of that wisdom is here between these covers, as well as the recipes to some of the drinks he's invented, and some he merely does well.

My advice, however, is to take the book directly to Amor y Amargo, order an Old Fashioned and read it right at the bar.

Sother will probably be there.

—ROBERT SIMONSON
Drinks and Liquor writer for The New York Times

AN INTRODUCTION

Hello.
I'm Sother Teague.

If the salutation above registered in your brain as some kind of written Johnny Cash impression, we're going to get along just fine. If instead you thought, "That's a great name for a bartender," then at the very least we can agree I was born to write this book.

If neither of those thoughts entered your mind, then the first thing you should know about me is this: I'm not prone to hyperbole. The second thing you should know is I've spent my entire working life in the service business.

I got my start in the industry at an early age. My dad owned a beachside bar in my hometown, and I'd carry cases of beer up from the cooler in exchange for quarters I'd immediately plunk into the bar's Missile Command or Centipede arcade machines. In hindsight, this was a pretty good deal for my father. From there I shucked oysters at a local dive and, as a man can only shuck so many oysters before he starts to question how he did God wrong, I fought the urge to say "shuck this" and instead transitioned into the role of line cook. I quickly learned I liked the feel of a kitchen, the ordered chaos and ordained spontaneity. With a firm grasp on my destiny, I decided to pursue a career as a chef.

"I'm not here for your life story," you may have just said aloud. "I'm just here for the drinks. That's the book's name. Why the hell am I reading about oysters?"

I suppose you've got me there. The recipes start on page 14, and if you're ready to get after it, you're more than welcome to skip ahead. But because who we were informs who we are (and because who I am defines the drinks I create) I thought it'd be helpful to at least tell you a little about where I came from. In fact, for much of this book I'll be doing something similar: defining a spirit and its origin story before introducing some of the delicious things you can create with it.

Which is to say, after working my way through school and paying my dues in several establishments, I was tapped to become the research and technical chef for the popular Food Network series *Good Eats*. When that opportunity led to a chance to be an instructor at the New England Culinary Institute, I jumped at the chance.

Then, quite by accident, I found myself behind a bar. It wasn't a tough transition—the pace and the mechanics are similar to being in a kitchen, and both offer an opportunity to create. But the bar also offered the added element of service—interacting with each guest and being as much a part of their experience as they'd like. Some just wanted me to set their drink down and walk away. Others—the majority in fact—wanted to engage in a conversation, either about what they were drinking, or how I made it. They wanted history, information, anecdotes. And I didn't always have the answers. As a former educator, this was a problem. To fix it, I started poring through books, scouring local libraries, watching and talking to other bartenders and experimenting with drinks at home. I got a little smarter. I got a little better. I got a little drunker, all in the name of being better at my job. I loved it.

Though I still cook things from time to time, I no longer feel I belong in the kitchen. The bar is my home, but I approach making cocktails the same way I did cooking food: Keep things simple, coax out flavors that are already inherent and present them humbly. It's a take that's been largely successful (after all, I'm now officially a published author).

Over the course of my career, I've spent innumerable hours behind all manner of bars in New York City, arguably one of the toughest places in the world to ply the trade. I've slung pints and slammed shots at the dirtiest of dives, paired wine with Michelin-star cuisine and crafted classic and new-wave cocktails at some of the most prestigious places on the planet. No matter the location or the variety of the drinks on offer, there is a constant that has informed my approach throughout my career: It doesn't matter if the drinks are good when the service is bad.

The handwritten "employee manual" at my bar, Amor y Amargo, has a paragraph that reads:

"We don't sell the lighting that we keep at the right levels based on the time of day and we don't sell the music that we keep at the right tempo and volume based on the amount of people in the room. We also don't sell the books, bitters and barwares that line our retail shelves. We certainly don't sell the well-thought-out and simply but beautifully presented cocktails and mixed drinks that we serve night after night. Our guests know they can get all (or most) of these items literally right next door. What we do sell is hospitality. All the aforementioned comes included in the price. And I want it to be a bargain that guests are happy and excited to pay us for again and again. It seems to work to everyone's advantage."

Now, this isn't a book about service. It's about drinks. And drinking. But the way in which I've structured it is, in some ways, still about service. The culture that has sprung up around mixed drinks, though it has afforded me accolades and some measure of success, is part of the problem. In an effort to establish bartending as a legitimate career choice, many in the trade have taken to calling themselves "mixologists," and half as many have taken to employing a uniform of the past in an effort to add future legitimacy. But in addition to the arm garters and waistcoats and waxed mustaches (all of which served the purpose of nodding to the history of our noble profession), a number of my peers have also taken on an air of "greater than." For them, the bar functions both as a place to ply a trade as well as a wall that separates those in the know from the people with whom, in my opinion, they're meant to share knowledge. Recipes are becoming more and more involved, with compound ingredients and obscure liqueurs and garish garnishes flown directly from the far east to satisfy the growing appetite for

"Come visit me at work. Tell me I sent you."

one-upmanship in the west. All of this is awesome in its own way. But it's also intimidating—if a customer can't pronounce anything on the menu, they'll have a tough time ordering a round. So, in the spirit of service (and in the service of spirits), I offer a slightly less involved approach. I believe cocktails can be complicated—but drinking them doesn't have to be. Making them doesn't either.

What lies ahead in these pages are guidelines for making delicious yet relatively simple drinks. Most will feature ingredients you can find in any liquor store, while others have a secondary recipe that'll send you from the bar to the kitchen. You'll learn how to make syrups, shrubs and even your own bitters-and-booze-infused marshmallows. But, as my approach to mixology is largely one of simplicity and straightforward technique, even these sub-recipes are pretty easy to master. That said, if anything herein appears too difficult, skip it, or better yet, keep taking cracks at it until your skills rise to the level of your ambition. If that doesn't work, just swap out or skip the element of the ingredient list you can't find (or don't want to make) and plow ahead. Some of the most lasting cocktails in the established canon were created under the exact same circumstances.

Every drink has the potential to be your new favorite and the ones that miss the mark will arm you with new knowledge on how to map your way to greater success. And if you get stuck, you can always reach out to me @creativedrunk on Twitter and Instagram. If I'm not making drinks at the office, I'll be happy to respond as best I can. There's also plenty of information to be mined on my weekly podcast, *The Speakeasy*, on Heritage Radio Network. Alternatively, come visit me at work. Tell me I sent you.

TERMINOLOGY & METHODOLOGY

A short primer on words and techniques I'll be throwing around a lot over the course of this book.

DRINK SERVICE CALLS

UP
Chilled over ice and strained into an empty stemmed Cocktail glass.

DOWN
Chilled over ice and strained into an empty Rocks glass.

ON THE ROCKS
Served over ice.

NEAT
Unchilled and poured into a glass with no ice or adornment.

INGREDIENT MEASURES

RINSE
In this context, a rinse is the act of coating the inside of a glass with a small layer of a specific liquid (ex: absinthe rinse).

SPLASH
A rough measurement typically indicating "a little," in the industry most bartenders interpret "splash" to mean one quick button-press of the soda gun. As you probably don't have a soda gun at your home, a good tactic is to tip the vessel in question (soda can, seltzer bottle) just enough for liquid to come out, then stop.

DASH
When referencing tincture bitters, a full turn of the bottle and two downward shakes, so that a "dash" of liquid comes out. "Two dashes" would be four shakes. I apply this as my standard as it allows for "half dashes."

DIFFERENT TYPES OF ICE
You can freeze or shape water into nearly any shape you like. If I say "with ice," I mean whatever ice you have on hand. If I suggest a specific type of ice, this is what I mean.

PEBBLE
Also called "pellet" ice, these are tiny, cylindrical pieces of ice used most often in tiki drinks. They are great for high-proof drinks because they melt quickly and dilute as you imbibe.

CRUSHED
Crushed or chipped ice is larger pieces of ice that have been crushed, either by a machine or by hand. They are great for Juleps because it creates a sno-cone effect and stays frosty until the last sip.

OVERSIZED OR LARGE FORMAT
These are big cubes of ice, typically 2 inches on all sides. You can purchase ice cube trays that make these "king cubes" at most retailers. They are great for straight pours or all-spirit cocktails because they melt slowly and do not over-dilute as you imbibe.

MIXING METHODS
The way you make your drinks is as important as how you plan to drink them. The below methods are the most common

BUILT
A cocktail that's made and mixed in the vessel (a glass; a cup; a coffee mug) in which it will be served. Old Fashioneds and Hot Toddies are built drinks.

STIRRED
A cocktail that's built in a mixing glass, then stirred with ice to chill and dilute before serving. These drinks are typically spirit-forward and usually do not feature any juice. The Martini, Manhattan and Negroni are all stirred drinks.

SHAKEN
A cocktail that's made in a shaker,

vigorously agitated with ice to chill, dilute, aerate and emulsify before serving. These drinks typically are brighter and more refreshing and feature juices, dairy, egg whites and/or other non-spirituous ingredients. The Daiquiri, Cosmopolitan and Pisco Sour are all shaken. I employ three shake styles in this book.

STRAINED OR DOUBLE STRAINED

Shaken and poured through a Hawthorn strainer (or poured through a Hawthorn strainer as well as a fine mesh strainer) to catch the remaining ice and/or stuff like pulp and seeds and other things you might have added for flavor but that you wouldn't want to drink.

DIRTY

Shaken and poured into the glass without separating the ice from the cocktail. Typically used for sours like the Margarita.

WHIP SHAKE & DIRTY POUR

A whip shake combines one set of ingredients with a small amount of pebble ice and is shaken vigorously until the ice completely melts to both aerate and chill, followed by a dirty pour as outlined above. It's typically used in tiki-style drinks.

BLENDED

A cocktail that's made in a blender. These drinks are typically lower in ABV, but are also larger in terms of their portion size. A frozen Margarita is a blended drink.

ROLLED

A cocktail that's made by combining the ingredients in one vessel with ice, then pouring it into another vessel, back and forth, to mix the drink. These drinks are typically more

TASTING TERMINOLOGY

When discussing spirits, it's typical to note how sweet or not sweet (aka "dry") a drink is. Something that is "off-dry" or "semi-sweet" is considered to be in the middle of the two extremes.

DRY   OFF-DRY/SEMI-SWEET   SWEET

GLASSWARE

In truth, you can drink pretty much any of my cocktails out of anything you like as long as it doesn't have a hole in it. That said, when I reference specific glassware, this is what I mean.

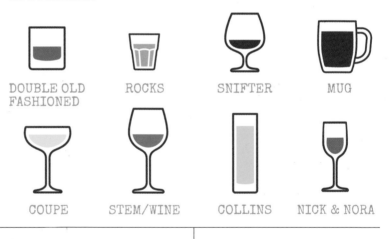

DOUBLE OLD FASHIONED   ROCKS   SNIFTER   MUG

COUPE   STEM/WINE   COLLINS   NICK & NORA

viscous or heavier, and need a bit of mixing but not so much that you want them to be aerated. A Bloody Mary is often a rolled cocktail.

THROWN

A cocktail that's made by combining the ingredients into one vessel with ice, then pouring it into another vessel, back and forth, to mix the drink—only this time you use a strainer to keep the ice in vessel #1. It's a way of adding texture as well as a moderate amount of aeration

to a drink, and is the least common method in this book (and real life). But that doesn't mean you should ignore it. Try throwing your next martini to create a drink with a unique texture.

SWIZZLE

A cocktail that's built in a glass with pebble ice and then agitated using a swizzle stick, which chills, dilutes and aerates the drink, as well as adds a little frost to the sides of the glass. All my swizzles are swizzles.

"Vodka is like water, but with consequences."

—Tom Rachman

ON VODKA

A primer on the spirit that begat all others—sort of.

I don't typically reach for vodka when I'm working on cocktails.

It's odorless, flavorless and might be the most contentious of all spirits. Both Russia and Poland claim to have invented it, there's an ongoing (relatively redundant) debate about whether grain or potato or beet-based vodka is superior and, despite being the second most popular spirit in the world, it's also among the most reviled by mixologists. Does it hold a well-deserved seat in the pantheon of spirits? Absolutely. But many (including myself) feel it doesn't belong in the cocktail conversation.

As such, it's a bit odd for me to kick off this, my cocktail book, with an entire section devoted to the stuff. But it's also difficult to discuss my approach to drinks and drinking without first talking about it—plus my editor said I had to, so here goes.

Vodka is the starting point for all spirits—sort of. Technically "beer" is the beginning of all spirits (again, sort of, which is why I put it in quotes. I'll explain in a bit). To understand what I mean, first consider the process of distillation. Or don't. Skip the next few paragraphs if you already know the basics of how wheat, corn, potatoes or pretty much anything organic becomes delicious, intoxicating alcohol.

When you distill something, you're heating it until it starts to vaporize, then capturing that vapor in a narrow vessel until it becomes liquid again. Ever heard of distilled water? Sure you have. It's water that's clean and pure and essentially the opposite of standing water in a pond somewhere. And that's because of the distilling process. Water has a lower boiling point than most of the contaminants or minerals it might contain (things like bacteria, sulfur, salt, calcium and—most likely—garbage and fecal matter). When you distill it, you heat the water until it boils and turns into clean steam, which you then capture and cool until it's water again, leaving all the stuff that didn't boil—all those impurities—behind. You'll have a little less than when you started, but you'll know it's safe to drink.

Just as salt and phosphorous and used Band-Aids have a higher boiling point than water, water has a higher boiling point than ethanol, meaning if you boil a pot of liquid containing both, the ethanol will evaporate first. So where does the ethanol come from? From the "beer" I mentioned earlier. What does this have to do with why I don't like vodka cocktails? I'm getting there.

The "beer" I keep bringing up is "distiller's beer," which is created through the process of fermentation. What's fermentation? It's the glorious chemical reaction that has kept me employed for more than three decades. It's a completely natural process where yeast (or other bacteria) consume the sugars of an organic product, such as grains or potatoes. Luckily for us, this creates two byproducts: gas (typically CO_2) and alcohol. If you trap the process in an airtight container, you'll generate carbonation. That's how beer is made.

Anything organic can be fermented, and anything fermented can be distilled. The first step is taking the grains (or whatever) and fermenting them in a vessel of water with some yeast, a little heat and a little time. Then, voilà—you've created distiller's beer or "the wash" or "mash." Is it alcoholic? Yes. Is it drinkable? Yes. Is it beer? Not necessarily, as it lacks a key ingredient, hops, which you would have added to your wash if creating marketable beer was your end goal. But, we're not. We're going to phase two: distilling.

The not-quite-beer is run through a purifying mechanism called a still—hence the name of the process. Just like distilling dirty pond water, this process separates the aspects of the liquid we want (the booze) from those we don't (the water) through selective boiling and condensation. The liquid that comes out on the other end of the process is considerably higher in alcohol by volume (ABV) because all the water has been removed. It's also cleaner, as it's been purified by the process. It's now a "neutral spirit." It's odorless. It's flavorless. It packs a wallop. It's essentially extra strength vodka.

The mind-blowing thing is this is how all spirits begin. To create something other than vodka, distillers will then macerate botanicals into the distillate to make gin, or age it in barrels to make whisk(e)y or start with a fruit-based mash to make brandy. But to make a bottle of vodka they'll just dilute it with water to lower its alcohol content (to approximately 40%) then bottle it up. Sure,

some run it through the still a few more times or filter it through charcoal to further purify the end product, but at the end of the day those are marketing gimmicks put in place to help the vodka taste more and more like nothing at all.

Most of the vodkas on the market are made from grains or potatoes but there are several made from other sources such as beets, sugar and even milk. I think this is interesting as trivia, but also kind of pointless, as the process of distilling renders the flavors inherent to the initial product all but obsolete. I don't see this as a bad trait for the spirit, but when we start to design cocktails around it, we run into trouble. Vodka has volume but very little substance, meaning it doesn't bring much to the party besides its alcohol content (which means it's still definitely invited to the party).

Examine the simplest vodka cocktail, the Screwdriver: 50% orange juice and 50% vodka. It's essentially a watered down, boozy glass of OJ. Is there a market for it? Of course. Is it a particularly interesting drink? Not to me, and to illustrate why, I'm going to stop talking about cocktails and start talking about food. If you were planning to make a soup from scratch, would you begin with odorless, flavorless water, or would you start with something like chicken or vegetable stock? If you said water, that's cool, but you're wrong. As a former chef, nine times out of 10, I'd start with some kind of stock—it's already got a flavor of its own upon which I can build and layer more flavors. I believe in following the same principle behind the bar when I'm designing a cocktail. You can start with milder base spirits like Old Tom gin, white

A copper still used for making both vodka and gin. Copper is an excellent conductor of heat and also naturally removes sulfides from the distillate, making it the most popular choice for spirit production.

rum or even blanco tequila, but the point is to start with something with a little flavor of its own. By design, vodka has none. It's just boozy water—its name is actually derived from the Russian for, you guessed it, "water."

As a result, I don't stock vodka at many of the bars I oversee. I don't stock it at my bar at home either, but that's not because I refuse to keep it on hand. Rather, it's because I store my vodka in the freezer where it belongs, ensuring it'll be as cold as possible when I serve it—the way it's meant to be served—and I won't have to dilute it with ice in order to cool it down. I don't like to add ice to vodka when I can avoid it. Consider that Screwdriver I mentioned earlier and then add the prospect of ice—which will always melt into more water eventually. You're lowering the alcohol content of your cocktail by adding water

(just like the vodka producers did when they added water after the distillation process). This isn't necessarily a bad thing; bartenders dilute cocktails intentionally all the time. But there's no reason to dilute a Screwdriver—it's meant to pack a bit of a brunch-boosting punch. And there's no reason to dilute vodka—it's vodka: boozy, 80-proof water. Why cheat it out of its true identity by watering it down with ice? As such, I always keep mine chilled. You should too.

As mentioned, I rarely mix vodka into cocktails (though I've included a couple classics here for you to tinker with), but when I do, I think of the legendary Japanese bartender Kazuo Uyeda, who says "Vodka is a celebration of the mixer!" as a guide to my approach. I also seek out concentrated flavors so they'll have greater impact when facing the volume increase

Fluffy Screwdriver

The Screwdriver is a simple blend of 50% vodka and 50% orange juice. A go-to for the early tee time set, my grandfather called it "aiming fluid." But to me it's a bit boring, as neither of the two ingredients really benefits from the marriage. The flavorless vodka just adds volume, and the result is watered down, boozy orange juice (you've read this rant before). Given that there isn't much to improve or tweak in terms of the ingredients, you can play with the methodology to add dimension and new texture to the drink. Noted barman Naren Young of NYC's Dante inspired my preparation. At his bar, they serve the Garibaldi: half Campari and half orange juice. Ingeniously, he peels oranges down to the white pith and pushes the whole orange through a Breville high speed juicer at the time of order. The result is a juice that is fluffy and silky, as if it were shaken with egg whites—if you've ever had an Orange Julius, the texture will be familiar. My preferred method is to peel the oranges in advance and use the peel for making oleo (pg 245) or as a garnish for other drinks. Keep the oranges in the fridge and the vodka in the freezer so both are cold when needed.

1 medium orange, peeled with pith intact

2 oz vodka

Push orange through high speed juicer. Put OJ and chilled vodka into a Highball glass.

Note: If you don't have access to a Breville juicer because you are a normal person who doesn't have a restaurant in their home, just peel the orange down to the pith and cut into small chunks, then toss them in your blender. Purée until smooth and strain through a fine mesh strainer before proceeding.

Garnish with an orange slice.

(read: dilution) brought on by adding the vodka: things like double strength tea or coffee, juice concentrates or homemade infusions, syrups or preserves.

Most of the time, though, I drink vodka in small, unadorned glasses, and I don't mix it with anything—except food. For me, the food is the mixer. Briny, salty or fatty foods are the perfect foil for the bracing cleanliness of chilled vodka. It's a solid choice when you're enjoying raw seafood like sushi, oysters or caviar and pairs beautifully with fatty pâté. But it's not solely for highbrow, frou frou food. I sip frosty vodka while munching on salt and vinegar potato chips or kosher pickles. Like all the spirits and cocktails in this book, your personal preference is going to play into this quite a bit, and if you like a Cosmo (to me, boozy cran-orange juice) or a Vodka Soda (to me, boozy bubble water) go for it. I can tell you all I know about cocktails, but you're the one drinking them; the only advice of mine you definitely need to take is to trust your own palette.

Moscow Mule

Spirits mixed with ginger ale or ginger beer and citrus are known as Bucks. And there's likely no more famous Buck than the Moscow Mule. In 1939, John G. Martin of the Heublein company acquired Smirnoff, a quintessentially Russian vodka that had relocated to France after the Bolshevik Revolution led to the nationalization of the vodka industry. The Heublein company made its fortune selling A1 steak sauce, and the vodka was such a dud in the States (where whiskey was the spirit of choice) that Martin nearly lost his position within the company. Legend has it while lamenting his plight to a friend at Hollywood's Cock and Bull restaurant, he added some of the restaurant's namesake ginger beer (which the restauranteur was also having trouble pushing out the door) to his vodka with a squeeze of lime and the result was magic. Dubbing the drink the Moscow Mule to further capitalize on the popularity of our post-WWII allies, Martin launched a national campaign to promote the drink.

He traveled the country with a copper mug and a Polaroid camera, photographing bartenders with the drink in hand. He'd leave them one copy to display on their bars and put another photo into a book that he'd carry along with him to show the next bar owner the popularity of the drink. As soon as the celebrity set caught wind of the drink it began to take hold nationwide. The Moscow Mule fell out of favor when communism and the Soviet Union became enemies of the state during the Cold War, but vodka's popularity was cemented by then. The drink has made an impressive comeback as well. The sharp bite from the ginger beer masks any burn from the booze, and the signature copper mugs make great housewarming gifts if you're into that sort of thing.

.75 oz lime juice

2 oz vodka

Ginger beer

Combine first two ingredients over ice in a copper mug. Top with ginger beer.

Garnish with a lime wedge.

I EXERCISE STRONG

SELF CONTROL

I NEVER DRINK ANYTHING

STRONGER THAN

GIN

BEFORE BREAKFAST

— W.C. FIELDS

Gin

jin / noun

1. a clear alcoholic spirit distilled from grain or malt and flavored with juniper berries and aromatics

2. mother's ruin

3. a card game, apparently

ON GIN

Yes, there's more to it than "it's flavored vodka...."

Let me start here: I love gin. Among my fondest memories of drinking gin are from two trips abroad. One was in the summer of 2015 when I took a long overdue vacation. In search of adventure and escape I ended up in San Sebastián, Spain, a part of the world I'd never visited. My original plan was to visit other cities in the region, and I'd even rented a car so I could. On my first day I wandered into a bar near my hotel and ordered a Gin and Tonic. It was an atypical order for me, but I try to adhere to a "When in Rome" attitude while traveling, and I knew the locals love their "GinTonics." With one drink order my plans for the week immediately changed.

This dive-bar Gin and Tonic in Spain beat every craft-bar version I'd ever tried. In America, we're making G&Ts all wrong: not cold enough, not enough ice and far too little tonic. Alternatively, this version was crisp, effervescent and refreshing.

The next day, like a man possessed, I went to a bar called La Gintonería, which boasts more than 100 gins and therefore over 100 GinTonics, each tailored with herbs, spices, citrus, bitters and tonics to match the botanicals of the gins. I spent my nights at the bar and days on the beach, where vendors would sell little paper cones filled with ham and GinTonics in plastic cups. It was a marvelous week. I never took the rental car out of the parking garage.

More recently, in 2017, I had a two-day layover in London, and having never been I wanted to pack as much as I could into a short trip. I reached out to my good friend Colin Asare-Appiah, a London native as well as a global spirits ambassador, who suggested a tour of the famed hotel bars in town: the American Bar and the Beaufort Bar at the absolutely stunning Savoy; the Connaught Bar and the Coburg Bar inside the beautifully appointed Connaught hotel; and finally Dukes Hotel to have a martini. Dukes, its bar, the martini and the bartender, Alessandro Palazzi, are all legendary. We were ushered to a table, where Mr. Palazzi rolled a bar cart tableside and entertained us with stories before elegantly preparing us perfectly dry, incredibly aromatic martinis. The heady aroma from fresh twists being pulled off massive lemons from the Amalfi coast filled the room. As an adult who's been jaded by the world, this was as close to magic as I've ever been. True hospitality and the company of a good friend with an exceptional martini in hand, it was a night I'll never forget, despite the number of martinis we consumed.

All of that is to say, I f*cking love gin. Integral to the business of making cocktails, it brings a lot to the table, with aromas that can range from slightly sweet (Genever; Old Tom); earthy (Plymouth); clean and bright (London Dry); to variously vegetal (most New Style examples). Every gin has a florality that's light and appealing and the flavors all feel like unique covers of the same incredible song. Gin appears in many classic cocktails, and I often reach for it when devising new ones.

But that doesn't really tell you what it is or where it came from, so for that bit let's start where we just left off a few pages ago, with vodka. As you no doubt learned and committed to memory, gin is essentially flavored vodka. The first time you put a barley and malt-made distiller's beer through a still, you create what's called malt-wine. It comes out of the still at approximately 50–55% alcohol, and its aroma and flavor are similar in aroma and flavor to new-make whisk(e)y, aka Moonshine—heavy with cereal grain and a malty sweetness. Keep distilling it and you'll get vodka. But you could also drink it then, though it's pretty harsh stuff, and not exactly palatable. In 16th-century Holland, distillers began adding a little juniper to their malt-wine during the distilling process and would distill it a second time. After adding a little water they ended up with a roughly 35% ABV spirit known as Genever or Holland's Gin.

Genever—which isn't exactly gin—is both the antecedent of gin as well as the missing link between gin and whisk(e)y. It was wildly popular until the late 1800s. Noted booze historian David Wondrich's research on the history of the spirit in the United States found that around 1850, the port of New York was receiving 4,500–6,000 120-gallon pipes of Genever per month (compared to only 10–20 of English gin) and "Professor" Jerry Thomas's seminal 1862 book *Bar-tenders Guide or How to Mix Drinks* calls for Holland's Gin in a great many recipes. So how did Genever get displaced by English gin? There are several theories, including that rye whiskey, somewhat similar in flavor, was more easily accessible in the States, and once the Martini was introduced to the imbiber's lexicon, Genever took another crushing hit as drier gins were more suited to mix with dry vermouth. Like whisk(e)y, Genever mixes beautifully with sweet vermouth. Some experts believe Genever gets short-changed when compared to gin and should rightfully be considered a flavored whisk(e)y, which could explain why I find it so easy to make cocktails that include both.

So how did Genever inform the creation of the gin we know today? Religion or war are usually the answer to history-based questions, and in this case it's both. Though Genever had been introduced to England as early as the 1570s, by 1618 the British were fighting alongside the Dutch in the Thirty Years War, the deadliest of the European religious wars. Armed with Genever—aka "Dutch Courage"—to aid in keeping morale high (as well to stave off illness from the cold damp weather), the Dutch had an advantage.

Soon enough, the Brits got their hands on a supply and quickly took a liking to it. Once the Dutch Prince of Orange became Britain's King William III in 1689, he boycotted brandy being imported from much-hated France, and as a result his spirit of choice, the Genever of his homeland, started making its way to jolly old England by the boatload. A year later, the London Guild of Distillers lost its monopoly on creating spirits, and soon would-be booze mavens throughout London and beyond began trying to replicate the most popular spirit in town.

They missed the mark. Their lack of experience making Genever (or any spirit, really), coupled with a lack of access to the ins and outs of the process led to a juniper-based spirit that started with grains distilled to a higher neutrality. Their end product, which became known simply as "gin," lacked the malty sweetness and multisyllabic music of the Dutch prototype. Some distillers, in an effort to get that Genever taste, started adding sugar to their mix, ultimately creating a spirit that came to be known as Old Tom gin.

Because of the proliferation of distillers and the prices of highly taxed imported spirits, consumption of gin increased rapidly in London at the outset of the 18th century in a period now referred to as the Gin Craze. Gin was cheap and easily accessible, making it the de facto vice of choice for the poor. And they drank it by the barrel. In fairness to the drinkers of the day, consuming more alcohol than one did water was particularly common, as even beer was safer for consumption than water. Still, to this day language allows us to decry gin when we mention unseemly bars as "gin palaces" or "gin mills" and when we refer to a drunkard as a "ginny" or being "gin-soaked."

During this era, gin quickly fell from grace. There were an estimated 7,000 private houses that made gin at the time, equaling one in four residences. This spurred moral outrage and led to legislation to try and slow consumption. Cost prohibitive taxes as well as stringent licensing were enacted to make it more difficult to get or serve the drink, which ultimately drove the practice into the underground market. Purportedly, pubs would hang a wooden sign of a black cat (an "Old Tom") on their outside walls to signify they were offering the illicit beverage. Some even installed a covert system for passersby to drop a coin into a slot, and through a series of lead tubes, they'd receive a shot of gin from the barman without having to walk into the establishment. Genius? Yes. A surefire way to get both alcohol and lead poisoning? Also yes.

But quality gin did receive government support. In 1793, in the maritime town of Plymouth, England—the Pilgrims' point of embarkation more than 150 years earlier—the Fox & Williamson distillery began officially producing what would become an iconic style of gin. Hallmarked by a natural sweetness attributed to the use of more roots in its botanical makeup, it's softer than London Dry but nowhere close to as sweet as Old Tom. In part because of the distillery's proximity to the sea, Plymouth became the "official" gin of the Royal Navy. New vessels were always equipped with a "christening kit" comprising a wooden box with two bottles of Plymouth and glassware for drinking. It was also available in what became known as Navy Strength, with an ABV of 57% or higher, in an effort to save precious space onboard a ship: Navy-Strength gin could be watered down without losing its punch. Plymouth, as well as other styles of gin,

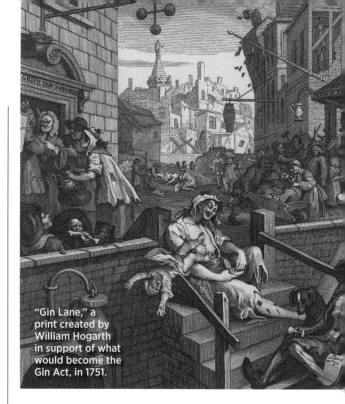

"Gin Lane," a print created by William Hogarth in support of what would become the Gin Act, in 1751.

can be purchased at Navy Strength today. It's also the gin of choice for the sailors' celebratory drink Mahogany: two parts Plymouth to one part warm treacle (that's molasses on our side of the pond).

Due to their constant desire for expedition and conquest, as well as their superior Navy, the Brits had a very influential role in mapping the world as we know it. And gin played a role in doing so. When soldiers were marching across India, malaria would strike them down in their tracks. The bark from the cinchona or "fever tree" contains quinine and was made into a tonic to reduce the fever and shaking associated with the illness. The tonic was incredibly bitter, so to help it go down, it was commonly mixed with gin. In other words, the Gin and Tonic powered the British Empire. Further, on long naval voyages, seafarers were often stricken with scurvy, a deadly vitamin C deficiency that a Scottish doctor named James Lind discovered could be combated through the consumption of citrus fruits. Sailors would likely have never made it to Australia had it not been for their gin and lemon juice, which is where the derogatory term "limey" is derived (the

The column still, developed in the early 1800s, revolutionized the production of spirits, and gave birth to London Dry gin.

word lime was used interchangeably for both types of citrus). As the empire expanded, one of the most important innovations in the world of spirits took place during the first third of the 1800s, which in turn led to another unique gin style.

The continuous or column still, patented by an Irishman named Aeneas Coffey, allowed for a greater speed of production of higher proof (and thus more neutral) spirits. Prior to the invention of the column still, all distilling was done using a pot still. Pot still production is on a batch-by-batch basis and, due to the nature of the still and its low-yield ability, the distillate maintains more of the wash's original flavors. The pot still can take the ABV of the wash from the initial 12–17% up to about 35%, meaning it'll retain more of the character of the wash, as is the case with Genever. Plymouth gin is still made using the pot still process. Alternatively, column still production is continuous, effectively distilling multiple times at once, resulting in less of the character of the wash at the end, as well as a significantly higher ABV.

And so, with the invention of this process, what we today call London Dry gin came into its own. It's got a crisper aroma that typically includes notes of citrus peel in addition to the required juniper. London Dry includes more botanical ingredients than Plymouth and Genever, and can include anise, caraway, coriander, cardamom, lavender and more. It has a much lower amount of added sugar, which is why its name includes the word dry. It also has the most regulations associated with its definition, officially established by the EU in 2008. London Dry is the largest category of gin and dominates the market share as far as sales are concerned. But there's a new style that's coming on strong. In fact, in some circles it's literally called "New Style."

No one seems to agree what to call this category (variations include New Western Dry, New American, International Style and New Style), partly because they're still all over the map. These are gins that go beyond the traditional palate of botanical ingredients and add flavors unique to each brand. All are still required to maintain a discernible juniper backbone as the base of their recipes (they're still gins, after all), but beyond that the distillers can experiment with whatever flavor profiles suit their needs. Examples include DH Krahn Gin, which includes galangal, a rhizome similar to ginger; Hendrick's Gin of Scotland famously adds rose petals and cucumber to their aromatics; Whitley Neill Gin adds cape gooseberries as well as notes of pear from African baobab fruit. Many of the New Style gins will operate using both a pot still and a column still to create their distillates, and will then combine the two after the fact.

The botanicals are added to all gins either as part of the mash, where they will be distilled, or are suspended above the mash in a "gin basket" (essentially a tea bag hanging above the wash) that all the vapor passes through on its way to the condenser. Some gins, referred to as compound gins, are made by creating a nearly neutral distillate and literally tossing botanicals into it to macerate, like you might do with a tea, before being strained out prior to bottling.

So now that I've taught you (almost) everything I know about gin, what should you do with it?

Drink it, obviously. It's not made to polish silverware. Genever, with its malt rich aroma and flavor is traditionally consumed neat from a small tulip-shaped glass filled to brimming, often with a lager beer as a chaser. Further, you aren't to pick up the glass at first because it's so full. Instead, bend at the waist and take the first sip opposite your drinking companion so that your heads almost (or actually) touch. This is called "kopstoot" and means "headbutt." Jonge Genever is delicious in lighter style cocktails like a Highball or Martinez, while the oude is more suited to cocktails like the Holland's Old Fashioned (pg 71) or mixed with rich ingredients like apple cider. Old Tom gin is the obvious choice for a Tom Collins, and it's what I reach for when I'm trying to coax a vodka drinker into a new realm of flavor possibilities. It's also great in a sour with lemon and honey. Plymouth Gin is my go-to for a Gibson. My friends and I often traipse across the city in search of the best Gibson, and though it largely relies on the quality of the pickled onion, for me Plymouth is the standard-bearer for the gin component. I also adore this gin for sipping on the rocks with a dash or three of bitters.

For a bracing martini, there is no substitute for London Dry gin, and my desert island choice here is the mighty but humble Beefeater. Nothing makes me feel more like a man of means than having a steak and a 50/50 martini for lunch. London Dry gin can also find its way into myriad cocktails ranging from the Negroni to the Bramble. New Style gins offer up so many opportunities for experimentation that it's tough to tell you where to begin. Hendrick's in a Southside is a no-brainer as the cucumber in the gin is bolstered by fresh cucumbers in the drink. Just don't fall into the trap of sticking to only one gin. The characteristics of each category, and each distiller's take on them, are different and worthy of attentive exploration. And you can't fully explore them by reading....

Five Gin Styles and Their Governing Principles...

Genever

A blend of two distillates: malt wine (a whiskey-like triple distillate made of corn, wheat and rye) and a juniper-infused distillate. Some distillers will also add a malt-wine that's been re-distilled with different added botanicals. By law, Genever can only be produced in certain regions: Holland, Belgium and small areas of France and Germany. Outside of the designated appellation, spirits of this sort must be labeled "Genever style." The terms jonge and oude are not a reference to the spirit's age, but denote the new or old style of making Genever: No more than 15% malt wine and 10 grams of sugar per liter for "young" and at least 15% malt wine and no more than 20 grams of sugar per liter for "old."

London Dry Gin

Must be made exclusively from ethanol of agricultural origin, and the botanicals—of which juniper must be the main component—must be introduced exclusively through re-distillation in traditional stills. They must be at least 70% ABV and may not contain added sugars exceeding 0.1 grams per liter of the final product. Additionally, no colorants or ingredients other than water are allowed. The term London Gin may be supplemented by the term "dry," but, interestingly, these gins don't need to be made in London, or even England.

Old Tom Gin

A slightly sweeter, maltier gin that was nearly lost to time, Old Tom has since been resurrected by distillers like Hayman and Ransom. There are no regulations governing its style and no clear rules determining its make—just as it was 300 years ago when it first gained popularity.

Plymouth Gin

This style gin, officially the oldest designated expression of the spirit, has been distilled using the same blend of botanicals since 1793. A proprietary blend of juniper berries, coriander seed, orange and lemon peels, green cardamom, and angelica and orris roots, each play a role in the blend, and are distilled with pure grain alcohol and soft water from nearby Dartmoor reservoir. The city of Plymouth, England, was once a Protected Geographical Indication, meaning it was the only place Plymouth gin could be created, but since the Plymouth distillery is the only one in town, the designation was deemed redundant in 2014.

New Style Gin

These are essentially gins that break all the rules—at least those governing London Dry gin. Where LDGs are juniper-centric, New Style Gins feature a wider (and occasionally wilder) variety of botanicals, which in turn inform their flavor profile.

Classic COCKTAIL

THE Martini

The Martini has become the epitome of what we know a cocktail to be, partly because the "Martini glass" has evolved into the de facto base ingredient for hundreds of cocktails across the globe (see: tini, Apple-; tini, Chocolate-; tini, Razzmatazz-). However, this iconic drink—the actual Martini—eschews some of the things most people associate with what a cocktail is. It has no juice. It is not shaken. It's also suffered from a pretty severe identity crisis due to the misunderstandings surrounding what vermouth is and how much of it should be used.

Vermouth is aromatized, fortified wine—a wine flavored with herbs and given a boost to its alcohol by volume with the addition of spirit. It's sort of a cocktail in its own way. Early versions of the Martini were mostly vermouth, as the gin was much higher in proof and harsher in flavor. The vermouth, in other words, took some of the stank off. As we got better at our distilling practices, we started needing less and less vermouth. But a peanut butter and jelly sandwich without the jelly is just a peanut butter sandwich. Still, you can overdo it on the jelly, so measure your vermouth to taste.

Sother Says
I prefer my Martini to be a 50/50 (meaning half gin, half vermouth) and always with a dash of orange bitters. But if I spy that the bar has a nice pickled onion, I go for a Gibson every time.

WATCH ME MAKE THESE DRINKS AT
VIMEO.COM/CREATIVEDRUNK

The Martini

A clean, crisp cocktail with as many devotees as detractors. Both are right.

2 dashes orange bitters

1.5 oz Dolin dry vermouth

1.5 oz London Dry gin

Stir all ingredients with plenty of ice in a large mixing glass to both chill and dilute. Strain into a chilled Cocktail glass.

Garnish with a lemon twist.

The Gibson

It's amazing what a pickled onion can do. With tartness salinity and a killer crunch, it defines the Gibson, among my favorite drinks of all time.

1 oz Noilly Pratt dry vermouth

2 oz London Dry gin

Stir all ingredients with plenty of ice in a large mixing glass to both chill and dilute. Strain into a chilled Cocktail glass.

Garnish with a cocktail onion.

Dirty Martini

More savory than a Gibson, with considerable amounts of salt and brine, the dirty martini is among my least favorite drinks of all time.

.5 oz olive brine

1.5 oz Dolin dry vermouth

1.5 oz London Dry gin

Stir all ingredients with plenty of ice in a large mixing glass to both chill and dilute. Strain into a chilled Cocktail glass.

Note: Most folks who order a Dirty Martini want it with extra olives, so I garnish with three by default.

BOND.
LAME BOND.

It's my contention that a classic Martini (which is to say one with gin) is the first "white Manhattan." Both follow the same rules of spirit, vermouth and bitters. Both are stirred drinks served up. Ergo, for me, the Martini is just a variation on the Manhattan.

It's a lovely, lively drink, yet many have never tasted one in the manner in which it was meant to be served. As such, a lot of people are of the opinion that they dislike Martinis.

I blame James Bond. Smooth as the spy may be, his oft-repeated drink order set a template for truly dreadful drinks, but that hasn't stopped it from being repeated by would-be Bonds the world over. For starters, 007 ordered vodka Martinis. The Martini isn't a vodka drink—it's a gin drink. The "vodka Martini" has its own name: the Kangaroo (3 oz vodka, 1 tsp French vermouth). As we've established, vodka is colorless, odorless, flavorless, neutral, distilled spirit. A cocktail comprised of vodka and vermouth simply tastes like thinned out vermouth. It lacks the delightful botanical zip of a Martini made with London Dry gin. However, this isn't the most egregious mistake Bond makes. More depressing is his famous direction: "shaken, not stirred." When a drink is made from all alcoholic ingredients, it should be stirred—this makes it cold and diluted without aeration, giving it a lush texture and more robust flavor. A shaken drink is less bold, with tiny air bubbles in temporary suspension so it dances across your tastebuds.

Consider the daiquiri. If you stirred one, it would taste powerfully sour—the lime juice would be in direct contact with your tastebuds. A shaken daiquiri, on the other hand, is a delight to drink. Bond's shaken "Martini" of colorless, odorless, flavorless, neutral distilled spirit and a touch of vermouth—already relatively bland in terms of flavor—is rendered basically tasteless. I'm not implying Ian Fleming didn't know any of this; he was known to drink entire bottles of gin on a daily basis. It's my belief Bond enjoys the effects of drinking as opposed to the flavor. His oft-quoted "shaken, not stirred" request is the spy's way of having his cake and drinking it too. That doesn't mean you have to. If you've never had one, give a true Martini a try.

Finally, James Bond is a fictional character. Why are you ordering a real drink "created" by a fake character? If you came to my bar and ordered a cocktail "invented" by Shrek, I'd be likely to show you the door.

Summer Rain

Plymouth Gin is the backbone of this refreshing tipple, but the Amaro Montenegro, with notes of orange blossom and bitter orange combined with a lush mouthfeel, is the hero, bolstering the role of juice in this recipe.

    Ginger and lime give it a real snap, and the cucumber and celery bitters offer a fresh, savory quality. Altogether it has a bright, wet aroma reminiscent of cool rain on a balmy afternoon, but you can enjoy it during any kind of weather.

SYRUP MADE SIMPLE

Simple syrup is a one to one ratio of sugar dissolved in water. You can further augment your syrup by steeping flavor agents in the water as you simmer. For example, add cinnamon sticks to the water for cinnamon simple syrup or vanilla beans and black peppercorns for a more complex syrup if complexity is your bag. You can also substitute some or all of the water with other liquids that already have flavor, such as apple or ginger juice. You can even use bitters.

    Syrups can be made from just about anything that has a distinct taste, which makes them a great vehicle for incorporating flavor into cocktails. For maximum impact with minimal dilution, most of my syrups are two parts sugar to one part liquid (also referred to as "heavy syrup"). For my ginger syrup, it's best to use fresh ginger juice as the liquid component rather than simply steeping ginger in the simmering syrup. If you don't have a method for juicing fresh ginger, go to your local juice bar and have them do the heavy lifting for you. Your efforts will be rewarded.

    If you're planning to make enough syrup to last a while (which you should if you're going to the trouble of making syrup in the first place), I recommend adding 1 oz. per quart of overproof spirit to the cooled mixture to extend its shelf-life.

Dash Bittermens Celery Shrub

3 thin slices cucumber plus one for garnish

.75 oz lime juice

.5 oz ginger syrup (pg 244)

.5 oz Amaro Montenegro

1.5 oz Plymouth Gin

Vigorously shake all ingredients (reserving one slice of cucumber) with plenty of ice to break up the cucumbers. Double-strain into a chilled Coupe glass.

Garnish with a thin slice of cucumber floating on top.

Sother Says

For a lower ABV variation, simply omit the gin and increase the Montenegro to 2 ounces. That's Spring Rain.

Giovanni Pompelmo

Old Duff Genever gives this refreshing Collins a subtle note of maltiness that's followed closely by the juicy appeal of both the Cocchi Rosa and Aperol, tied with a nice bow of grapefruit bitters and lengthened by seltzer.

One of the added benefits of this drink is that with the exception of the grapefruit twist, it's made up of non-perishables, making them easy to have on hand to make at a moment's notice. It's juicy and bright without any juice and is impossibly refreshing.

2 dashes grapefruit bitters	1 oz Aperol
1 oz Old Duff Genever	Seltzer
1 oz Cocchi Rosa	

Pour first 4 ingredients into a 10-oz. Collins glass and add ice. Gently stir to cool. Top with seltzer.

Garnish with grapefruit twist.

Sother Says
Make it a royal by substituting sparkling wine for the seltzer.

Negroni

As is common among classic cocktails, the true origin of the Negroni may forever remain a mystery. It revolves, it seems, around two different men named Negroni, both claiming to be Counts, though only one definitely held the title. The most widely accepted tale takes place at a small cafe in Florence, Italy, in 1919 when (alleged) Count Camillo Negroni ordered "an Americano with gin." The drink is also credited to General Pascal-Olivier de Negroni, definitely Count de Negroni, who allegedly invented the drink in Senegal some 60 odd years prior to Count Camillo. Equal measures of London Dry gin, sweet vermouth and the iconic bitter Italian aperitif Campari, common components in bars all over the world, make it easy to remember and replicate. Bracing and tinged with slight bitterness of burnt orange, it's either served on the rocks or chilled and served "up" with an orange twist (sometimes flamed) or slice of orange. My specification on the Negroni takes a slight detour from the original. I forgo the equal parts in favor of a more gin heavy 2:1:1 ratio.

1.5 dashes Angostura bitters	
1 oz Campari	
1 oz sweet vermouth	2 oz London Dry gin

Classic COCKTAIL

Build all ingredients in a rocks glass. Add one large format ice cube. Stir to combine.

Garnish with an orange twist.

Sother Says
Doubling the gin helps with dilution. I offset the loss of bitterness by adding Angostura.

Secret Service

This is a pretty simple riff on the Negroni, which you hopefully just read about unless you're jumping around. Maurin Quina is a fortified wine that's bittered with quinine and sweetened with cherry juice. Here it's playing the role of sweet vermouth while the subtly smoky and slightly spicy Ancho Reyes subs in for the Campari. Cinnamon and cocoa notes work in concert with both of those and all are standing on the foundation of herbs from the gin.

2 dashes mole bitters	.75 oz Maurin Quina
1.5 oz Plymouth gin	.75 oz Ancho Reyes

Pour all ingredients into a mixing glass and add plenty of ice. Stir to chill and dilute. Strain into a rocks glass filled with fresh ice.

Garnish with an orange twist.

Singapore Prospers

Often, when I'm manning the bar, guests will ask for cocktails that are "Like a *enter classic cocktail name here* but not a *repeat classic cocktail name here.*" This was the case when I created Singapore Prospers.

The flavors in this cocktail are meant to mimic some of those in the iconic Singapore Sling while still honoring the no juice ethos of Amor y Amargo. Instead of London Dry gin, we've substituted a blend of Old Tom (a sweetened gin), with Genever (a malty gin predecessor). In lieu of the Cherry Heering, we incorporate the lush juiciness of Carpano Antica sweet vermouth with Burlesque bitters (açai berry, hibiscus and long pepper). Dry Curaçao and lime bitters round out this spiritus and delightful tipple.

1 dash Bittermens Burlesque Bitters	.5 oz Dry Curaçao
	1 oz Carpano Antica
3 dashes Scrappy's Lime Bitters	1 oz Genever
	.5 oz Old Tom gin

Combine ingredients into a mixing glass and fill with plenty of ice. Stir to chill and dilute. Strain into a Rocks glass over fresh ice.

Garnish with an orange twist.

Blackberry Julep

1 oz fresh lemon juice

1 oz Marie Brizard
Blackberry liqueur

1.5 oz Hendrick's Gin

Shake the ingredients with ice and
strain into a Highball glass filled
with crushed ice. Stir until the glass
begins to frost.

*Garnish with a tablespoon of
marinated mixed berries (pg 245) on
top of the drink and a mint sprig.*

Few other careers offer you the opportunity to meet your idols as readily as bartending. Even during my years as a cook, it was difficult to just walk up to chefs and start chatting with them because they're in the back of the house. Bartenders, on the other hand, are right there behind the bar and happy to strike up a conversation—it's part of the gig. I don't recall the exact first time I met legendary bartender Dale DeGroff; that's likely due to the fact that he has such a way of putting you at ease. Even the first time you meet, it seems like you've known him for years. As time has passed, I've been extremely lucky to have cultivated a true friendship with him, and I value it dearly. Dale's hospitality is peerless, and his spirits knowledge is unparalleled. Winner of two James Beard Foundation awards as well the founder of the Museum of the American Cocktail, he is largely responsible for the mixology revolution that has, ultimately, led to you reading this book. They don't call him "King Cocktail" for nothing.

When I solicited a few recipes for inclusion in the book from my friends and peers in the industry, his was the first response, and it's a lovely addition. "The Blackberry Julep was a drink I created for Blackbird Bar Restaurant in New York City on East 49th Street," says Dale. "The restaurant only lasted one year, but it was a special one, giving me the opportunity to finally hire Audrey Saunders, a woman I met some years earlier when she was ending a marriage, leaving a successful business and starting a new life behind the bar. I was impressed for a lot of reasons, but none more than her courage to completely reinvent herself in mid-life." Saunders would go on to open New York's Pegu Club—one of the most storied cocktail bars in the city.

The drink itself is a sipper that'll withstand all seasons, but I recommend it most from late spring to early fall, when fresh berries are in season. As an added bonus, the marinated berries recipe for the drink's garnish is the same one utilized to create the topping for the Baked Alaska served at the Rainbow Room supper club 65 floors above Manhattan, where Dale began to gain international acclaim behind the bar.

Waterproof Watch

Anybody who's even remotely into cocktails should know the name Dale DeGroff (and you should too since he was mentioned in the previous recipe). Both silver haired and silver tongued, he's a mentor to us all in the craft of making drinks as well as the art of tending to guests. I'm lucky to call him a friend.

Dale started producing his own line of bitters a few years ago, and they are exceptional. Full of baking spice flavors and sharply bitter, Degroff's Pimento Bitters have become an essential on my bar (Pimento is the island term for the allspice berry). They're also the ingredient that makes the Waterproof Watch tick. Aperol's grapefruit flavors combine with orange notes in Montenegro to make a drink that's incredibly juicy without the addition of any actual juice. Dale's bitters bring it all home with a hint of spice and bitterness to finish. This cocktail is, for me, a summertime sipper, but you're welcome to consider it anytime you like.

2 dashes Degroff's
Pimento Bitters

.75 oz Amaro Montenegro

.75 oz Aperol

1.5 oz London Dry gin

Stir all ingredients with plenty of ice in a large mixing glass. Strain into an Old Fashioned glass with fresh ice.

Garnish with an orange twist.

A PROPER TWIST

A twist can make a massive difference to any cocktail. Please note: A twist is not a slice of lemon; a twist is not a wedge of orange; a twist is a twist—a section of peel that is twisted (hence the name!) in order to express the oil from the peel onto the drink's surface. Because oil is thicker than water, the oil expressed from the peel will rest on the top of the drink and impart flavor via aroma throughout your enjoyment of the drink itself. My weapon of choice for twists is a straight peeler, which I use to seperate the peel from the rest of the fruit. I try to avoid as much pith (that white stuff) as possible, while still keeping the twist thick enough to squirt when I squeeze it.

I HEART BITTERS

There once was a time when bitters were relied upon just as much for their traditional capacity to cure ails—ranging from liver spots and baldness to cancer and impotence—as for their use in cocktails. In fact, we get the term "snake oil salesman" from early vendors who'd roam from town to town with a wagon full of vials and sell them to the locals before disappearing in the night, headed to the next burg of potential rubes ready to pay top dollar for what were, essentially, aromatic bitters. There were hundreds of so-called tonic bitters on the market at the turn of the century. However, when the FDA was established in 1906, the Pure Food and Drug Act was passed, prohibiting interstate commerce in adulterated and misbranded food and drugs. The upshot of this legislation was that items, including bitters, could promote all manner of claims on their labels, but only if they could be backed up. Most could not, and bitters went from the pharmacy to the liquor cabinet virtually overnight. Those bitters that made no medicinal claims (only claims of deliciousness), such as Angostura and Peychaud's, persevered. More than a century later there's been such a renewed interest in tincture bitters that many bars are well stocked with numerous brands.

So what exactly are bitters? To me, they're the grout between the tiles that make up a cocktail. They're the seasoning in the soup. The only time you should notice them is when they aren't there—when your cocktail is just a little off.

All bitters are built from three main components: alcohol, bittering agent and flavor agent. Alcohol is always the base, serving as a solvent and facilitating the extraction of flavors from the bittering and flavor agents. There are many bittering agents, and each producer can use whichever ones suit their recipe. They include but are not limited to roots, barks, flowers, herbs, fruit peels and seeds. Common bittering agents are cassia, quinine, gentian, angelica and wormwood. Finally comes the flavor agent. The possibilities with this component are seemingly endless. To wit, on my bar I have everything from hibiscus to Sriracha flavored bitters.

Making bitters is a deceptively simple process. Using the highest proof spirit you can get your hands on, steep your ingredients like you would a tea for several days or up to several weeks. Strain out the solids and add some water to attain the desired proof and flavor profile. I recommend anyone who's truly interested in making craft cocktails go through the process at least once, if only to learn the effort, time and money aren't exactly well spent—even if the resulting product tastes good. Unless you're meticulous with your process and note-taking, it'll likely be impossible to repeat. Plus, a more consistent version of whatever you're trying to create likely exists because professional bitters artisans have done all the leg work. There's a satisfaction in doing something yourself. There's also something to be said for kicking up your feet and letting someone else do the heavy lifting.

Flight Deck
with Aviation

FLIGHT DECK

2 dashes 18.21 Ginger Lemon Tincture

.5 oz fresh lemon juice

.25 oz Maraschino liqueur

1 oz Becherovka

1 oz Monkey 47 gin

Shake all ingredients together with ice. Strain into a chilled Coupe glass.

Express the oil from a lemon twist and use as garnish.

AVIATION

1.5 tsp Crème de Violette

.75 oz fresh lemon juice

.75 oz Maraschino liqueur

1.75 oz Beefeater Gin

Shake all ingredients together with ice. Strain into a chilled Nick and Nora glass.

Garish with a Maraschino cherry.

Classic COCKTAIL

This is a playful riff on the Aviation, a classic cocktail comprising gin, Maraschino liqueur, Crème de Violette and lemon juice (the Crème de Violette is integral to achieving the pale blue hue reminiscent of the sky and sparking the drink's name), which first appeared in print in 1916.

Becherovka is a cinnamon and clove liqueur from the Czech Republic that's balanced between bitter and sweet. Often I've heard it referred to as "Christmas in a Glass." For the gin, I'm moving to another category, New Style, meaning that in addition to the legally required juniper and the list of common botanicals necessary to be called gin, they incorporate some unorthodox ingredients. In this case, blackberry, nutmeg and licorice are all present, among many others—Monkey 47's name is derived from the fact that they boast 47 botanicals. Those flavors combine nicely, creating a harmonious balance from two spirits hailing from neighboring countries. The ginger lemon tincture seasons the whole thing and punches up the aroma considerably.

One sip and you're ready for takeoff!

INTRO TO LIQUEURS

Liqueurs are generally made from distilled spirits that are flavored with all manner of fruits, nuts, creams, herbs and spices. Typically they're pretty low in alcohol by volume (though some are as high as 55% like the famously monk-made Chartreuse). I think of them as alcoholic syrups. As a result, liqueurs are rarely the foundation of a cocktail as they're often far too sweet. In fact, most classic cocktail recipes rely on them as tertiary ingredients (ex: The Aviation or Margarita [pg 150]). That said, I do find some liqueurs can be a delightful finish to a great meal, though only if they're offered in the proper diminutive glassware.

Ramos Gin Fizz

3 drops orange flower water

.25 oz simple syrup

.5 oz fresh lemon juice

.5 oz fresh lime juice

1 fresh egg white

1 oz heavy cream

1.5 oz gin

Seltzer, chilled

Combine the first 7 ingredients in a shaker without ice and shake vigorously to combine. Add ice to the shaker and shake again for at least a couple minutes (more if you have it in you). Strain into a straight-sided glass, top with seltzer and stir.

No garnish.

No list of classic gin cocktails would be complete without including the Ramos Gin Fizz. The unlikely pairing of gin and heavy cream results in a pillowy meringue with a perfume of orange blossom. This is the very architecture of skilled bartending. For me the RGF is a breakfast or brunch drink, but it's easily enjoyed anytime.

COCKTAILS WITH EGGS

Rocky isn't the only guy who enjoys drinking raw eggs; there's a decent chance you have as well. Eggs pop up in a variety of cocktails ranging from fizzes like this one to sours, flips and nogs. Egg whites are added to cocktails to add a creamy texture to the body of the drink as well as form a foamy head on top. Fresh egg whites are essentially flavorless and odorless in their raw state, so they go undetected in the final product. Egg yolks come into play to add richness and an almost buttery flavor to drinks like the Golden Fizz (not often called for these days). The whole egg comes into play in drinks such as Eggnog or the holiday favorite Tom and Jerry (typically these drinks also contain dairy). There are also Royal Fizzes that contain whole eggs and no dairy and benefit from both a rich body and foamy head with the addition of flavor from the yolk. As long as the eggs are safe to eat, they're safe to drink.

Overcast Beach Day

It's common practice in the cocktail world to borrow ideas from the existing canon and reshape them into new forms. Overcast Beach Day is an example of this method. Here I've combined the methodology of the classic Ramos Gin Fizz (pg 46) with the playful flavors of a Piña Colada. I'm preferential to the herbal quality the gin lends to the drink and encourage you to try it as is before moving on to other spirit choices.

2 drops orange flower water

.5 oz pineapple juice

.5 oz orange juice

.75 oz coconut milk

1 small egg white

1.5 oz Plymouth Gin

Seltzer

Add first 6 ingredients to a shaker tin with plenty of ice and shake vigorously for at least 45 seconds to chill, dilute and emulsify. Strain into a straight-sided, 8-oz. glass. Allow to sit for another 45 seconds (I usually put the glass in the freezer during this rest period). Then, gently and slowly pour in 2 oz. of seltzer.

If all goes well, it'll rise above the rim of the glass like a meringue.

No garnish.

SHAKE IT

There are at least three methods for shaking cocktails with egg whites and each has a unique result (my recipe for the Overcast Beach Day features a reverse dry shake).

STANDARD SHAKE

Add the egg white to your ingredients and ice in a cocktail tin and shake vigorously for at least 30 seconds before straining over fresh ice into a Rocks glass. This will result in a beautiful, foamy head.

DRY SHAKE

Add the egg white to your ingredients without ice and shake for 30 seconds to start an emulsion. Add ice and shake for at least 30 more seconds before straining into a cocktail glass. Let the drink rest for 30 more seconds prior to serving. This will result in a smooth foamy head stable enough to "paint" with bitters, etc.

REVERSE DRY SHAKE

Add the egg white to your ingredients with ice and shake vigorously for 30 seconds. Strain the mixture back into a cocktail tin and shake again for 30 seconds without ice prior to pouring all contents (no need to strain) into a straight-sided glass. Allow to rest refrigerated for 30 to 60 seconds prior to gently pouring seltzer into the center until the head rises above the glass. This method will result in maximum foam.

Lazy Dessert

I was in search of relief on a hot Brooklyn night but didn't have much on hand. I did, however, have half a pint of mint chocolate chip ice cream—and I'm never far from a bottle of gin. The bracing nature of minty ice cream combined with the herbal quality of gin is a no brainer for me. If you'd like to take it to the next level, don't skip the Brancamenta. I haven't since that first summer night.

2 oz mint chip ice cream (softened)

1.5 oz London Dry gin

.5 oz Brancamenta (optional... if you're feeling lazy)

Add to a shaker and whip to combine. Add a metal straw and drink directly from the shaker tin.

No garnish.

GinTonic

In Spain, they claim to have invented the GinTonic, represented as one word. Whether that's true or not, they've certainly elevated the simple highball to cultural phenomenon status. While in America we typically drink a concoction of roughly 3 parts gin to 1 part tonic, which results in a boozy, non-effervescent tipple garnished meekly with a lime wedge, the Spaniards' ratio is more the opposite, resulting in crisp effervescence that stands in refreshing contrast to the former. Further, it's ritualistically assembled even at the most dive-y of bars: First, a thick-bodied goblet is chilled and gin is added, then ice is piled in and the gin is stirred to chill. Another layer of ice is added and juniper berries are dropped into the glass, with more stirring. Still more ice and finally cold bottled tonic is gently added with a final swirl to incorporate.

Classic COCKTAIL

2 oz gin

4 oz tonic

Add gin to a chilled Goblet. Add ice and stir. Add more ice, and top with tonic.

Garnish as you desire.

Bees Knees

This is a simple sour recipe that never fails to impress. It's my go-to when I'm introducing someone to gin, as it's pleasing to the palate with familiar flavors of honey and lemon. If you're imbibing on a cold winter night, try the drink as a hot cocktail and float cold cream on top.

.75 oz honey syrup

.75 oz fresh juice

1.5 oz London Dry gin

Classic COCKTAIL

Shake with ice. Strain into a chilled Cocktail glass.

No garnish.

> **Sother Says**
> You can swap out the lemon for lime juice to make the Business cocktail.

Eastside Fizz

Spring and summer deserve a cocktail like the Eastside Fizz. For me, the very name conjures up images of a cold Collins glass beading with sweat, effervescent bubbles racing one another to the top where cucumber slices and mint leaves await. This is another in an ongoing list of sour variations that's lengthened with seltzer. A tall glass of cucumber water is thirst quenching in its own right, but here we punch it up with bright mint and herbal gin. The addition of seltzer gives the drink life and vibrancy.

2 slices cucumber

8 mint leaves

.5 oz heavy syrup

1 oz lime juice

2 oz gin

In a shaker, muddle mint and cucumber. Add remaining ingredients and shake with ice. Double strain into a Highball glass filled with ice. Top with seltzer.

Garnish with mint and cucumber.

THE Clover Club

.75 oz fresh lemon juice

.5 oz raspberry syrup
(if you prefer a bit fresher
and drier, simply use 4–6
raspberries and 1.5 tsp
of sugarfine sugar)

.75 oz aquafaba

1.5 oz gin

Combine ingredients in a shaker and shake without ice for 10 seconds. Add ice and shake vigorously for at least 10 seconds. Double-strain into a chilled Coupe glass.

Garnish with raspberries.

Named after a men's club in Philadelphia, the Clover Club has proved wildly popular since its inception in the early years of the 1900s. The club was primarily made up of men of means who used their financial power to create jobs and engage in charitable acts. Though the cocktail faded out of the limelight due to Prohibition, it's been enjoying a renaissance for several years. Herbal London Dry gin combines with a sweet tart syrup of fresh raspberries and sharpness is supplied by a dose of fresh lemon juice. The technique here is to really give the shaker a run for its money. The classic Clover Club was made using egg white to get that lovely, marshmallow-y head. But for this recipe I've swapped out the egg white, which I recognize some people find off-putting, with aquafaba (the liquid you find in cans of chickpeas), which I also realize some people might find off-putting. Like egg whites, aquafaba is largely odor- and tasteless, and whips exactly like its less-vegan friendly counterpart. Plus, it practically eliminates the possibility of foodborne illness in your cocktails—trust me, that's a win. The generally agreed upon rule of thumb is that one tablespoon of aquafaba is equal to one yolk, two tablespoons is one white and three tablespoons is a whole egg. Once shaken into the cocktail (or whipped into food recipes) it is virtually undetectable.

AQUAFABA: WHAT IT IS, WHEN TO USE IT

Aquafaba (Latin for "bean water") refers specifically to the liquid in canned chickpeas. During the cooking process, water soluble carbohydrates and proteins leech out into the liquid, resulting in an ingredient with functional properties that mimic those of egg whites. I know the knee-jerk reaction is to think your cocktail is going to taste like hummus, but, similar to egg whites, it's relatively odorless and flavorless. The great news for cocktail lovers is aquafaba has a much greater shelf stability than egg whites—you can have a can of chickpeas on hand at all times. The fact that it's vegan certified makes it appealing to an even wider audience. You can use it just as you do egg whites, with roughly .5 oz standing in for each one. And it's not just for cocktails. Aquafaba can stand in for eggs in a number of recipes. It can whip up like meringue, emulsify dressings and even be turned into mayonnaise. It doesn't fare well in custards, though.

Red Gin
with Pink Gin

I'm a huge fan of Pink Gin (it's just Plymouth gin and a heavy dose of Angostura bitters after all. What's not to like?) but, I'm also an aficionado of the Old Fashioned cocktail (pg. 70), and that's exactly what Red Gin is: Spirit, water, sugar and bitters.

For the spirit, I prefer a bold London Dry gin and a workhorse that's always in reach: Beefeater. I encourage you not to turn your nose up at this stalwart—it's well made and affordable and as reliable as the sunrise. If you've turned your back on it, give it a revisit and see if your tastes have changed.

The water and sugar are in the form of a syrup here: the grenadine. It's easy to make and will last quite a while in your refrigerator. Plus, it'll be better than almost anything you can conveniently purchase because it'll actually have pomegranate in it.

As for the bitters, Peychaud's works better for this recipe than the standard Angostura because it has a kick from cinnamon as well as a soft hint of anise. Plus, it stays on target with the namesake color—or so they tell me (like 11% of the male population, I'm red-green colorblind).

RED GIN

3 dashes Peychaud's bitters

0.25 oz homemade grenadine (pg 245)

2 oz London Dry gin

Splash of seltzer

Combine all ingredients into an Old Fashioned glass. Add ice and stir a few times to combine.

Garnish with a lemon twist.

PINK GIN

4 dashes Angostura bitters

2 oz Plymouth Gin

Dash the Angostura into an Old Fashioned glass, then roll it around to coat the inside. Add the gin, then stir. That's it. Drink up, sailor.

No garnish.

Agua DE Fresa

When they're in season, strawberries are as delicious as they are eye catching. Just the sight of a plump juicy strawberry excites the mind with possibilities. This drink was inspired by a summer salad of peppers and strawberries in a lemon and herb vinaigrette. Here, the gin takes the place of the herbs and the Verde steps in for the peppers. A kick of vinegar from the shrub completes the illusion. The juxtaposition of sweet, spicy and slightly savory keep the palate excited, making this "strawberry water" go down as easily as its name implies.

.5 oz fresh lemon juice

.5 oz strawberry shrub (pg 245)

.5 oz Ancho Verde

1.5 oz London Dry gin

Seltzer

Shake first 4 ingredients with ice and strain into a Collins glass filled with ice. Top with seltzer.

Garnish with a strawberry.

Burning Love

Fresh thyme sprig

.5 oz Génépy des Alpes

.5 oz lime juice

.5 oz Maraschino liqueur

1 oz Plymouth Gin

Place thyme into a heavy Rocks glass and pour in Génépy. Pour all remaining ingredients into a shaker tin with ice. Using a long match or torch, light the thyme on fire. Shake the tin as the thyme burns. Pour the shaker's contents, ice and all, over the burning thyme to extinguish the flames.

Garnish with thyme sprig.

Fire is always an intriguing element in cocktails both because it's visually stunning and because it creates layers of flavor and aroma in a unique and immediate way. The aroma of fresh thyme burning in a pine liqueur conjures up memories of fireside cocktails in the lodge after a day of skiing. Further, it adds a layer of char to the final concoction. Maraschino liqueur is the distillate of the cherry pits removed for making the classic maraschino cherries (not to be confused with the bright-red American version). The liqueur is clear in color and straddles the line between sweet and dry with the slightly almond flavor of marzipan. You can't make the iconic Hemingway Daiquiri (pg 174) without it. Here, it assists in balancing all the herbal notes from the other components.

AROMA = FLAVOR

Ever notice how when you're sick with a stuffy nose that food generally tastes like cardboard? That's because aroma and flavor are intrinsically linked. Your tongue only perceives five flavors (sweet, salty, sour, bitter and umami or savory), but your olfactory sense (nose) can detect thousands of aromas. As we consume foods and beverages, we simultaneously smell them, increasing our perception of flavor. So, by expressing the oil from a citrus twist over a cocktail, muddling the leaves of an herb or charring items, we expand our ability to perceive aromas, thus increasing our ability to enjoy the cocktails!

Try this at home: Make your favorite cocktail that involves a twist but stop before expressing the oils over your drink and smell and taste the cocktail. Then proceed with the twist and smell and taste again. Dramatic change!

TOO MUCH
OF ANYTHING IS BAD BUT TOO MUCH GOOD
WHISKEY
IS BARELY ENOUGH

— MARK TWAIN

Whiskey

(h)wiskē / noun

alternative spelling: whisky

1. a spirit distilled from fermented wort (such as that obtained from rye, corn, or barley mash)

2. firewater

3. in the NATO alphabet, W

The Manhattan, pg 74

ON WHISK(E)Y

Staying true to our core analogy, whiskey (or whisky, if you're in Canada, Scotland or Japan) is simply "vodka" made from a "beer" of fermented cereal grains—most commonly wheat, corn, barley and/or rye—and typically aged in brand-new, charred barrels from either American or European oak. Unlike their counterparts in the vodka industry, whisk(e)y distillers aren't aiming to create a neutral, odorless, flavorless spirit—they distill in a way that allows the distillate to retain a bit of the wash's flavor, a cereal grain scent that is refined or evolves completely over the course of the aging process.

The great thing about American whiskey is that unlike so many other categories, there are clearly defined rules and regulations defining production. This levels the playing field for comparison's sake, meaning unlike gin (where you're looking at different distillers who can add any number of botanicals to their distillate in order to influence its flavor) when you compare one bourbon to the next, you're comparing apples to apples. Er, corn to corn.

Given the space allowed, I'm going to stick mostly to American whiskey and touch on scotch whisky a bit later as I feel a deep connection to both, being an American of Scottish descent. I unfortunately don't have the space to dive too deep into Japanese, Irish or Canadian whisk(e)y (although I'd gladly swim in a vat of all three) except to say the Japanese make whisky in the Scotch style and are narrowing—and in some comparisons leaping over—the gap with

their counterparts in Scotland. The Irish have mastered the use of the pot still and have rebounded from the crash of the late 1800s, which stripped the country from 88 distilleries to only three. That number has since grown to 18, making Irish whiskey one of the fastest growing categories year over year since 1990. And, though I'll likely piss someone off, the entire Canadian whisky biz is built on a foundation of lies. When Prohibition began, those wily Canucks took advantage of their fellow North Americans' love for rye whiskey and started calling pretty much anything they distilled that was brown "rye"—even though it contained very little rye grains. This practice has gone unchecked for nearly a century. Do Canadians think we're stupid? Don't answer that.

Whisk(e)y is where I got my start as a drinker. My dad was an American whiskey drinker, and my granddad was a whisky man (they drank Jack Daniels and Cutty Sark, respectively). They were regular joes with modest tastes—a sensibility I still appreciate. To me, the scent of whisk(e)y is a homecoming. It may surprise even those close to me to learn I didn't have my first drink until I was 22 years old. A tee-totaling Straight Edge as a youth, I rebelled against my parents by not participating in their chosen habits. But, at 22, I tried my first beer: a Guinness. My first experiment with the harder stuff was Absolut vodka, neat, and I drank it that way for more than a year. But then I found whisk(e)y. I'm not lucky enough to remember

A barrel of Rye whiskey aging at George Washington distillery, Mount Vernon, Alexandria, VA.

my first, but, I know by the time I was 24, I was drinking Old Overholt almost exclusively. We used to call it Old Overboard, Old Overthrow or Old Overbite because we were obviously hilarious. I didn't know how to describe it then; I only knew I was (am) in love with American whiskey. As it turns out, America's forefathers were as well.

Early colonists of America arrived after a long sea voyage and found themselves running out of the supplies they brought along with them. Namely, they were low on spirits and completely out of beer. Consuming water—packed with dysentery-dishing microorganisms—wasn't as common a practice as it is today, and beer was the primary source of hydration. Beer also served as a ready source of nutrition and calories for energy so, win-win? To deal with their lack of beer supplies, the settlers looked around and saw maize, or corn. They started making beer with it and likely distilled some into an early version of corn whiskey. A variety of local ingredients were also tested—because hey, you never know what might make a delicious beer. Would-be beers and distillates of the era included experiments with berries, plums, potatoes, apples, carrots and other grains such as rye. As we formed the Continental Congress, George Washington himself had a distillery at Mount Vernon. He started

selling unaged whiskey in 1797 after getting the idea from his farm manager. It was, at the time, among the largest commercial distilleries in the country. By 1799, the last year of his life, the distillery was one of Washington's most profitable endeavors.

Meanwhile, Scots-Irish and German settlers were setting up shop in western Pennsylvania and Maryland. They brought plenty of distilling know-how and even seed stock with them. The European barley they brought on the journey took some time to acclimate to the North American weather conditions, but the rye grains were hearty and adapted quickly. This spurred them to produce a spirit made with a mash bill of mostly rye. The spirits produced in these middle colonies became known as Maryland whiskey or Monongahela (the Monongahela River connected their trade routes), a precursor to modern rye.

In 1783, Evan Williams founded the first commercial distillery, in Louisville, Kentucky, on the banks of the Ohio River. In 1791, as a means to recover from the debt of the Revolutionary War, the first tax on distilled domestic spirits was levied. Because whiskey was the most popular spirit at the time, this effort was labelled the "Whiskey Tax," and led to a nearly four-year standoff known as the Whiskey Rebellion. In 1801, Thomas Jefferson became our third president by running as a member of the newly founded Democratic Republican Party in part because of his promise to repeal the tax. Whiskey went untaxed until 1812. In addition to taxing whiskey, the government enacted regulations on the production of spirits in America in order to have a clearer view of what and how much was being produced—most likely so they could levy and collect the proper taxes. They've been sticking it to imbibers ever since.

The upside of regulation, however, is that the government made it pretty easy to distinguish between the different American whiskey styles by dictating that each respective style must contain a minimum of 51% of the grain associated with that spirit. So, rye whiskey, rye malt whiskey, malt whiskey and wheat whiskey must contain at least 51% of their namesake grain in the mashbill.

The outlier here is bourbon, which must contain 51% corn. There are (as is nearly always the case with booze history) conflicting stories as to where bourbon got its name. First off, the idea that bourbon was named after Bourbon County, Kentucky, or that it must be produced there is completely false. In fact, Bourbon County had no operating distilleries from 1919 until 2014, when the Hartfield & Co. Distillery opened and started making small batch bourbon. They remain the only distillery in the county. While proving a fallacy doesn't necessarily reveal the truth, there are two tales of bourbon's etymology that are the most plausible. The Bourbons, the eventual French Royal family, were involved in trade between Kentucky and Louisiana. As they'd send their wares down the Ohio River, they'd label crates of goods and barrels of produce and whiskey with their name, Bourbon. As the spirit gained popularity, barkeeps would ask for it by that name. Similarly, the Tarascon brothers from the south of France in Cognac settled in Louisville in the 1870s. They knew from drinking Cognac that their fellow French expats living in New Orleans would appreciate spirits mellowed in charred casks and began shipping their experiments with this style down the river. Even back then, Bourbon Street was the hub of civilization in New Orleans. As the spirit began to gain renown, people would ask for "That whiskey they sell on Bourbon street" or "That Bourbon whiskey." Either way, the name stuck.

Digressions on bourbon aside, for all American whiskeys, it's up to the maker to decide what to include in the mashbill (beyond 51% of the grain required to earn the name they're going for) based on their desired outcome. The whiskey cannot be distilled to higher than 160 proof, ensuring it retains characteristics of the initial grain. Further, adding coloring or flavoring agents is prohibited. Though the government does not specify a minimum aging time, the process must take place in brand-new, charred American oak barrels. The barrels aren't cheap to purchase and can only be used to make whiskey once by law, so most makers get a return on investment by aging for at least two years.

Once the spirit has achieved a two-year mark of aging, it can be labeled as a Straight Whiskey. If the whiskey is aged less than four years, it may not state an age on its label. Adding an age is optional if the spirit has matured for more than four years, but many producers choose to put an age statement on the label as they're aware the public views them as an indicator of quality.

But older isn't necessarily better. In fact, many American whiskeys are less than four years old and are outstanding representatives of the category. Among them is my personal favorite, the aforementioned Old Overholt Rye, the longest continuously produced rye in the country. Old Overholt quietly makes delicious whiskey without advertising or price gouging, and was one of only six distilleries to be granted a medicinal license during Prohibition, meaning they could produce whiskey for a doctor to prescribe to patients (I'm sure many ailments for which whiskey was the only cure cropped up during the Noble Experiment).

Though there are a few outliers, the two largest categories of American whiskey are rye and bourbon, and the difference in flavor is clear. Rye tends to be slightly fruity with spicy back notes while bourbon is decidedly sweeter with a fuller body. To help you remember, think about the difference between rye bread and cornbread or the fact that we derive so much sweetener from corn in the form of syrup. It seems a little unfair that though rye has a longer history in the U.S., somehow bourbon took over as the more popular of the two; Congress even named bourbon America's Native Spirit in 1964.

Prohibition may have had a hand in bourbon's rise, but to understand why requires a deeper understanding of the era as a whole. The 18th

Amendment was ratified in 1919 and with the Volstead Act defining its rules, Prohibition was enacted on the first day of 1920. Yet much to the dismay of the government and supporters of Prohibition, drinking rates began to rise. In addition to a rise in alcohol consumption, crime associated with the underground business required to distribute it also increased, including bootlegging and the theft of industrial alcohol—stuff intended for use in paints, fuels and solvents.

During Prohibition, the government required all industrial alcohol to be denatured, rendering it undrinkable. But by the mid-'20s, approximately 60 million gallons of industrial alcohol were being stolen per year. The criminals responsible hired chemists to re-nature these spirits, rendering them safe(ish) to drink and would marry smuggled or illegally distilled booze they could get their hands on with watered down kerosene and industrial alcohol to make their supplies last.

By the end of the decade it's estimated there were 30,000 speakeasies in New York City alone. By comparison, there are only about 10,000 legal bars and restaurants that serve alcohol today. In the mid-'20s, alcoholism was soaring by more than 300% according to insurance company records of the time. The Noble Experiment was failing in spite of its ignoble practices. The government's response? Fight chemistry with more chemicals. Officials mandated that industrial alcohol should be more heavily tainted, and in 1926 the Treasury Department demanded more methyl alcohol be added, up to a deadly level of 10%. The theory was that if the public knew there was a chance the alcohol they were obtaining illicitly might be poisoned, it would deter them from drinking it. It didn't.

In late 1926, 1,200 people in New York alone were poisoned by bad booze. Four hundred of them died. The following year, the number of deaths rose to 700. By the end of Prohibition, it's estimated the government was indirectly responsible for upwards of 10,000 deaths, the vast majority being minorities and the poor. Making matters worse, many of those who died simply disappeared. If you were to fall

A Few Outliers in the Whiskey World...

White Dog

Also called raw whisk(e)y or Moonshine, every whisk(e)y ever made starts off as white dog. Whisk(e)y gets its amber color from the barrels in which it's aged. As you may have surmised, white dog is unaged and therefore is as clear as water. Distillers have found that in the past decade or so public demand for white dog has increased, leading to higher availability.

Bottled-in-Bond

Any U.S. whiskey may carry the label distinction of Bottled-in-Bond if it is the product of one distilling season from January to June or July to December and is made at a single distillery by a single distiller. It must be aged at least four years in a government bonded warehouse and bottled at 100 proof. This practice was introduced in 1897's Bottled-in-Bond Act following the widespread adulteration of American whiskeys. It's basically a government guarantee that what's on the label is what's in the bottle, and protects both the maker and the consumer from fraud.

Tennessee Whiskey

It seems a bit misleading to call Tennessee Whiskey an outlier as one of the most popular whisk(e)ys in the world, Jack Daniels, falls into the category, but, here we are. Tennessee Whiskey is a bourbon whiskey specifically made in Tennessee then filtered through a ten-foot layer of maple wood charcoal before being barrel aged. The filtering, called the "Lincoln County Process" after the county where Jack Daniels distillery was founded, imparts a sweeter, lightly sooty flavor and mellower final product.

Corn Whiskey

This whiskey must be 80% corn in the mashbill and does not require any aging. If it is aged it cannot be bottled at higher than 125 proof and, in an odd and confusing turn, must be aged in used or uncharred barrels. Several bourbon makers will also produce a corn whiskey so they can reuse those expensive barrels to generate more revenue. Mellow Corn, a Bottled-in-Bond corn whiskey that typically sells for less than $20 a bottle is currently having a moment in the mixology scene. Get it cheap while you can!

A crowded bar at one of New York's many speakeasies, 1933. Prohibition would officially end on December 5 of that year.

ill and die while at a speakeasy, you'd likely have been bundled up and disposed of by the proprietor, who couldn't run the risk of having their business shut down or facing jail time for selling alcohol in the first place (For this, and other reasons, I'm lukewarm on the romanticized aesthetic of the modern speakeasy movement).

All of this is a long way of saying that an official sense of higher purpose overtook some in our government's better judgement, and that the booze being served at speakeasies across the country was pretty harsh stuff—the result of government intervention and proprietors' improvisational ingenuity. As a result, cocktails became sweeter, and juices, dairy and eggs were used more and more in order to mask the bad taste of the alcohol, establishing many of the foundational elements for what we now view as classic cocktails. The creativity borne out of sheer necessity led to some of the most bulletproof recipes in the cocktail canon. After all, if you can make a deadly ounce or two of varnish taste good enough for your customers to order another round, there's a pretty good chance your recipe will be even better with unadulterated spirits.

Once Prohibition came to an end, the drinking habits (and tastes) developed over the nearly 13-year period remained. The palates of American imbibers were now conditioned to appreciate sweeter flavors, which helped bourbon overtake its spicier cousin rye as the whiskey of choice. It's been that way ever since, but I'm not about to let the preferences of a bunch of criminals who were willing to drink ethanol in order to get a buzz determine which spirit is superior. As much as I love bourbon, I generally prefer rye.

If I'm reaching for a rye to make an Old Fashioned (pg 70), it's going to be softer and lower proof so it doesn't burn my face off—and for me, that's Old Overholt. If I'm looking to make a Manhattan (pg 74) or a cocktail that's lengthened with lower proof or nonalcoholic ingredients I'll reach for a spicier rye with a bolder backbone of 100 proof, like Rittenhouse. As for bourbon, I adore Elijah Craig. At 94 proof, it's soft enough for an Old Fashioned or neat sipping while simultaneously brash enough to build a cocktail around. For the recipes included in this section, these are the bottles I use (unless otherwise specified). But you, like our whisk(e)y-loving forefathers, should blaze your own trail.

THE Old Fashioned

One of the first things you learn when you start researching a particular drink's origin story is that many have a blurry history, most likely based on the hazy memories of their respective imbibers. The Old Fashioned is one such drink. The Pendennis Club of Louisville is often credited with first serving the Old Fashioned in 1881, purportedly using bourbon made by James E. Pepper. Except they didn't. Robert Simonson debunked this ubiquitous claim in his book on the drink, explaining—among other things—the methodology of muddling the fruit as they do in the Pendennis version wasn't common for several decades.

The first sighting of a recipe for the Old Fashioned is in Theodore Proulx's book *The Bartender's Manual*, dated 1888, but they were undoubtedly ordered in bars before then. What we think of today as an Old Fashioned is not the "first" cocktail by any stretch, though its origin is the very foundation upon which most of today's cocktails are built. Despite establishing itself through a specific series of iterations, it continues to evolve.

Long before there were bartender's colleges and award-winning mixologists, there was booze. And generally, it didn't taste all that great. It was common to drink spiritus liquor with a bit of sugar and over ice, if you had any. The phrase "a spoonful of sugar helps the medicine go down" surely came from this practice. Bitters were also introduced, creating what became known as the cocktail, for which a definition was first printed in May of 1806 ("a potent concoction of spirits, bitters, water and sugar," according to the Hudson, NY, paper *The Balance and Columbian Repository*).

At this time the most common "cocktail" was made with rye, though as the definition suggests, any spirit was acceptable. The term "bittered sling" was also synonymous with the cocktail, as slings were simply mixtures of spirit and sugar with water, typically by half. Some years later, the cocktail underwent an "improvement" where creative bartenders added small amounts of liqueurs to the concoction and served the drink chilled but not on ice. First was the addition of absinthe and Maraschino liqueur to Genever, as in the Improved Holland's cocktail. By the late 19th century, the Sazerac, with its absinthe rinsed glass and featuring a dash of Peychaud's Bitters (bottled by the drink's creator, Antoine Amedie Peychaud)

had also arrived on the scene, with delicious results. Despite the growing popularity of these allegedly improved drinks, some folks weren't into absinthe—or any other "adulteration" to their spirits—and by the 1880s, it would have been commonplace to say you preferred your cocktail the "old fashioned way," hence the name. To put the notion into terms from the 1980s as opposed to the century prior, fancy/improved cocktails like the Sazerac were New Coke. Ordering an Old Fashioned was a cue to your bartender that you preferred Coca-Cola Classic.

Following the success of the temperance movement, Prohibition had a direct impact on the growth of the "Old Fashioned" as a drink, and not because people stopped drinking them altogether. Because liquor production and distribution were driven underground, the spirits available in the States were often adulterated and very rough to drink. They required more than a little sugar and bitters to tame them, and as a result, bartenders began muddling a slice of orange and a cherry to the mix, effectively making single-serving punch. The American taste for all things sweet helped this practice carry on even after Prohibition was lifted and better spirits were available, and in general, this iteration of the Old Fashioned has proliferated in chain restaurants and basement bars across the country.

But in my opinion, there's a better way, particularly if you're using quality spirits. I prefer the spicy but still smooth flavor from an 80-proof rye. I tend to go for Demerara syrup as opposed to granular sugar and rarely muddle a slice of orange in my Old Fashioned—I find that a proper twist is all I need. I skip the Maraschino cherry altogether because they give me the creeps. A solid ice cube and a double dash of Angostura come together to showcase why this throwback will always impress. But that's my way. As long as you adhere to the basic template of spirit, bitter, water and sugar, there is no end to the possibilities for an Old Fashioned-style cocktail. The Campfire Old Fashioned, an invention of my own, is an example of how the format can be bent to your will depending on the taste you're after (in this case, the smells and warmth of drinking whiskey by a roaring fire). There are other Old Fashioned riffs throughout this book, but these recipes—much like anything else—are what you make of them. And you should.

Bittered Sling

1 small sugar cube

2 oz spirit of choice

1 oz water

In a Rocks glass, crush a sugar cube with a muddler. Add your spirit of choice, and stir to dissolve the sugar. Add water and a lump of ice.

No garnish.

Classic Old Fashioned

Dash Angostura bitters

2 oz rye

Spoon demerara or cane syrup

Lemon twist

Add first 3 ingredients to an Old Fashioned glass. Add a large lump of ice and gently stir to combine.

Garnish with lemon twist.

Modern Old Fashioned
(Prohibition era)

Small white sugar cube

1/2 orange slice

Maraschino cherry

Dash Angostura bitters

2 oz rye

In serving glass, muddle sugar, orange and cherry with bitters. Pour in rye, add ice and stir to chill and combine.

Garnish with extra cherry and additional orange slice.

Improved Holland's Fashioned

2 dashes Angostura bitters

1.5 tsp of demerara syrup

4 dashes absinthe

4 dashes Maraschino

2 oz Old Duff Genever

Add all ingredients to a mixing glass with plenty of ice. Stir to chill and dilute then and strain into a chilled Cocktail glass.

Garnish with a lemon twist.

Sazerac

Absinthe or Herbsaint

2 dashes Peychaud's Bitters

.5 oz simple syrup

2 oz rye whiskey

Give a chilled glass an absinthe or Herbsaint rinse and set aside. Stir the other ingredients in a mixing glass, strain into the chilled glass.

Garnish with a lemon twist.

Campfire Old Fashioned

Dash Angostura bitters

Dash Bittermens Hellfire Habanero Shrub

1.5 tsp of cane syrup

.25 oz peated scotch

.75 oz rye

.75 oz bourbon

Add ingredients to an Old Fashioned glass. Add a large lump of ice and gently stir to combine.

Garnish with an orange twist.

Mint Julep

The Mint Julep is an incredibly humble drink. Sugar syrup, fresh mint and spirit over crushed or shaved ice is all you need. An early mention of the mint julep appears in a book by John Davis from 1803, where he described it as "a dram of spiritus liquor that has mint steeped in it, taken by Virginians of a morning." It's interesting to note Davis mentions the time of day and that the drink is "taken" as juleps were considered morning drinks or "fog cutters" and were thought to have medicinal properties. We can also guess by his mention of Virginians, who were in the habit of growing corn at that time, that the julep was likely made with bourbon, though other versions appear using Genever, peach brandy and other spirits. Some folks even used wine.

Whatever spirit you choose (Bourbon. Choose bourbon.), it should be 100 proof or above—a drink served over crushed ice will dilute awfully fast, leaving a lower proof spirit lost in the water. I use a 1:1 ratio for simple syrup here, which in turn helps balance the higher proof spirit. Spearmint is the only mint for a classic Julep, so save the chocolate mint, apple mint or other franken-mints for non-standard variations. Finally, this drink deserves a traditional nickel-plated Julep cup. Don't worry, they're not as expensive as the $1,300 sterling silver ones that are heirlooms in the South.

Classic
COCKTAIL

12-15 fresh mint leaves

1 oz simple syrup

Crushed ice

2.5 oz overproof bourbon

Superfine sugar (NOTE: Don't use powdered sugar)

Place mint and .25 oz of the syrup in a Julep cup or Old Fashioned glass and gently crush the mint leaves with a wooden muddler, working them up the sides of the glass. Loosely pack the glass with finely crushed ice, then add your bourbon. Drizzle the remaining syrup on top.

Garnish with mint sprig lightly dusted with sugar.

A WORD ON PROOF

Proof is the measure of the content by volume of ethanol in an alcoholic beverage. This measure is largely used by government agencies to tax the beverage, but there's some fun lore attached as well. Back in the 16th century, as a way of measuring the alcohol content of a spirit, a pellet of gunpowder would be soaked with the liquid. If it could be ignited, the liquid would be rated above proof and taxed at a higher rate. If the spirit was lower than 57.15% ABV, it wouldn't burn and was taxed less. Similarly, on Royal Navy ships, sailors were given a daily ration, or tot, of rum. If the rum bosun responsible for delivering the ration was thought to be over-diluting the tot, the gunpowder test was applied as "proof" that the rum was strong. Interestingly, the practice of daily tot was in use until 1970, when it was abolished due to concerns that daily intake of alcohol could lead to unsteady hands while operating the ship.

It's important to take notice of proof when building cocktails. Standardization has brought most spirits down to 80 proof, but classic recipes written prior to the turn of the century, were made with stronger spirits. For example, I build my Negroni with two parts gin to one part each of vermouth and Campari; the gin used in the original was likely well over 100 proof, so I add more gin to offset the dilution from the other, lower ABV spirits. In general, vermouth's rich and full bodied nature can overwhelm a spirit with a lower ABV, so I also choose to use higher proof whiskeys (90 or even 100) in my Manhattans to punch through it.

THE **Manhattan**

A personal favorite of mine, The Manhattan also has an uncertain origin story. It's another classic drink whose genius lies in its simplicity. Three common ingredients combine in harmony to make one superlative concoction. Each ingredient is equally important to the outcome. Is the vermouth elevated by the biting rye, or is the rye tamed by the herbal vermouth? It's difficult to say, but for me the dry baking-spice notes from the bitters bring it all together in perfect harmony. The Manhattan, and its variations (including the Martini, which I'd argue is simply a White Manhattan), are on my desert island drinks menu. And, as detailed below, my eats menu.

The key ingredient here is the sweet vermouth, arguably among the most misunderstood bottles on the back bar. Vermouth is simply aromatized, fortified wine. Aromatized with botanicals and bittering agents (the root word *wermut* is German for wormwood after all) the wine is then fortified with spirits. If you take a bottle of table wine and add diced pears and oranges and a few cinnamon sticks, you've aromatized it. Pour in some brandy and you've fortified it. You may not have made vermouth, but you've made its party-loving cousin Sangria. However, it's still wine, and should be treated accordingly. Refrigerate after opening and consume within a few days. Have Manhattans at your dinner party tonight, drink vermouth on the rocks with leftovers tomorrow.

2 dashes Angostura bitters

1 oz sweet vermouth

2 oz rye

Stir in a mixing glass to chill and combine. Serve up.

Garnish with cherry or lemon twist.

MANHATTAN GLAZED RIBS

My early career as a chef combined with my years behind the bar opened my eyes to flavor combinations I may have otherwise overlooked. In 2016, I was again invited to participate in the StarChefs International Chefs Congress, held yearly in Brooklyn. Though they invited me as a bartender, I asked if I could cook. Any chef worth their salt can make whiskey-glazed ribs, and I wanted to be unique. So, I made rye whiskey, sweet vermouth and Angostura glaze for my entry. A Manhattan glaze! It was incredibly successful as well as relatively simple to replicate. I paired them with my Martini Pickles, and you should too. Recipes on page 247.

Uppercut

I love a good punch. Not just because they are always a crowd-pleaser or because they are whimsical in appearance, but because they are nearly always delicious. I created this punch during a trip to Colorado. A group of friends and I were there for an event where whole pigs were being roasted, a long, slow process that gave us ample time to catch up over drinks. But none of us wanted to be shackled to the bar and thus, the Uppercut, a bold, batchable punch, was born. I recommend using a heavy-hitting bourbon like Wild Turkey, which at 101 proof can handle considerable dilution from the juices. Applejack provides a fruity foil to the mix as well. If you can locate Becherovka, an herbal liqueur from the Czech Republic, you'll immediately fall in love with its sharp notes of cinnamon and clove. If not, cinnamon clove syrup will do the job. It's a punch. You don't need to get too precious with it, and that's the whole point.

2 dashes Bar Keep Apple bitters

.5 oz lemon juice

.25 oz orange juice

.25 oz Becherovka (or cinnamon clove syrup, pg 244)

.75 oz Applejack

1 oz bourbon

Hard cider

Build in a glass over ice and top with cider. For punch, simply scale up the ingredients by the number of guests you expect to serve, allowing for two drinks per guest.

Garnish with sliced apples and grapes.

MAKE A BUNCH

Large format cocktails are a great way to serve a lot of people quickly, as well as free up the host for entertaining. When it comes to large-format imbibing, punch has the market cornered. For centuries, we've gathered around a flowing bowl to both celebrate and commiserate. Punch is originally derived from the Sanskrit word for "five," which describes the number of its components. There's even a nursery-style rhyme to help us remember the build of a classic punch:

One of sour,
two of sweet,
three of strong and,
four of weak.
A dash of bitters,
a sprinkle of spice,
serve well chilled
with plenty of ice.

Truthfully, this standard can be helpful in single serving drink design as well.

But punches aren't the only way to have substantial amounts of cocktails on hand. Consider the bottled cocktail. Any cocktail that doesn't involve perishables (juice, eggs, dairy, etc.) can be built in advance, bottled and chilled. I also recommend adding a little water to make up for the missing dilution from shaking or stirring (from 18%–25% of total volume). I always have a bottled Manhattan as well as a Martini tucked into my freezer for unexpected company or personal emergencies.

THE Breakfast Bell

This foamy drink has many of the flavors I associate with breakfast—maple syrup, coffee and hot sauce—which is why I like to serve it at daytime events and brunches. People are generally fascinated by the look of fizz drinks that include egg whites. They don't add much by way of flavor, but when properly handled, egg whites give the drink the texture of a fluffy meringue. The Breakfast Bell is like a sweet and savory milkshake. I like to serve it with what I call "the Bartender's Breakfast," a sidecar of the unused egg yolk topped with hot sauce and cracked pepper, taken as a shot. I was always bothered by what to do with the egg yolks left behind after making egg white cocktails, so I started offering this as a bonus treat. It's a more holistic approach to the usage of the egg and a tried and true hangover cure. Plus, it's delicious. *Ding ding!* Order up!

1.5 tsp B-grade Maple syrup

1 oz cold espresso or strong black coffee

1 oz cream

2 oz bourbon

Sriracha, to taste

1 egg, separated

Seltzer

Pour bourbon, espresso, cream and syrup into a shaker tin. Add in Sriracha to season to your taste. Add the white of an egg, reserving the yolk. Shake without ice to emulsify. Add ice and shake vigorously for 2 minutes. Strain into a chilled Collins glass and let sit (preferably in the refrigerator) for 2 minutes. Gently pour seltzer into the center, the foamy head should rise past the top of the glass like a meringue. Place the egg yolk into a shot glass with a dot of Sriracha and cracked pepper on top and serve on the side.

No garnish.

HANGOVERS HAPPEN

Let's take a second to acknowledge one of the realities of drinking for most people: the hangover. Drinking alcohol leads to dehydration, and when you're dehydrated your body's organs get first dibs on any water in your system. Your brain gets the shaft here, which is why one of the hallmarks of a hangover is a screaming headache. Additionally, as your body metabolizes alcohol, your liver also creates a substance called acetaldehyde, a toxin that increases headaches and causes nausea, which is why a night of heavy (and for some people, light) drinking usually leads to a morning where you feel like utter garbage. There are a number of hangover "cures", and most imbibers swear by one or another. Some stick to caffeine, others fatty food. There are also proponents of drinking more booze (aka the "hair of the dog"), which is why the Breakfast Bell is a solid post-party morning cocktail—the caffeine and the whiskey, with a sidecar of spicy egg yolk will open your eyes and settle your stomach. In lieu of an over the bar solution, you can try an over the counter remedy—Blowfish (*forhangovers.com*), at right, features a combination of stomach-settling agents, aspirin and caffeine to combat nausea, fight your headache and kickstart your day. Some of my regulars swear by the stuff, but I wouldn't know—despite drinking a well above average amount of booze, I don't get hangovers. Whatever you choose to fight your next-day blues, know that the best way to combat a hangover is to avoid one in the first place. That starts with matching yourself drink for drink with a full glass of water, which most bars will sell you for free.

SCOTCH WHISKY

A category, a culture and, for some, a way of life.

There's enough to say about scotch that I could easily fill an entire book. But for now, I only have the space to do a surface level exploration the category. Frankly, I'm pissed my editor made me waste all that space on vodka, because I, like Ron Burgundy, love scotch.

It seems obvious to state scotch whisky is malt or grain whisky made in Scotland, and while that's true, it's again just a surface level definition, and one that doesn't begin to speak to the variety within the category. Scotch is made in a manner similar to that of all whisk(e)y, with one notable addition: many scotch producers use heated peat briquettes during the drying of their barley, which imbues the whisky with what many would describe as its signature smokiness. The other difference between scotch and its spirituous cousins is that while there are a few regulations denoting what is or is not a bourbon or a rye, there are myriad laws governing the production of Scotland's pride.

Until the late 18th century, it was all made from malted barley, but since then wheat and rye grains have been added to the possible mashbill. Further, following a 1909 scandal of adulterated whisky sales, the Royal Commission redefined what scotch was and a century later, in 2009, additional requirements were imposed and incorporated, officially governing the entire industry. The Scotch Whisky Regulations dictate all mashing, fermentation and distillation must be done at the distillery, which must be—surprise!—located in Scotland. All scotch must be aged a minimum of three years in oak casks no greater than 700 liters in size. Aging must also be done in Scotland, though not necessarily at the distillery. Scotch must be bottled at at least 40% ABV, and any age statement on the label must reflect the youngest whisky in the bottle (this pertains to blends). Within those rules there are five different types of scotch, which also have their own rules and regulations.

Single Malt Scotch Whisky

Must be distilled at least twice in a copper pot still and made from 100% malted barley from a single distillery. This can be confusing, as it means one bottle of single malt may contain malts distilled at different times, but that's within the rules as long as they're from the same distillery.

Blended Malt Scotch Whisky

Formerly known as vatted whisky, this is a blend of two or more single malts from different distilleries.

Single Grain Scotch Whisky

Made by a single distillery but can include malted barley and any combination of un-malted cereal grains from a patent still. It's largely used in blends rather than being bottled as is.

Blended Grain Scotch Whisky

Utilizing two or more single grain whiskies, Blended Grain Scotch Whisky features a combination of whiskies from different distilleries using the patent still process.

Blended Scotch Whisky

By far the most popular category in terms of consumption, making up roughly 90% of global sales, Blended Scotch Whiskey is a blend of several different grain and malt whiskies. The proportions vary from producer to producer but usually, the malt proportion is around 25%.

One more thing to cover: There are also five different production regions for scotch, each of which—because of climate, production methods, soil and air quality—results in a unique flavor profile for the end product. Like I said, scotch could use its own book. But here we are. Since I'm limited on space, I've presented the five regions as well as my "If I could only have one bottle from this region" selection for each. Thankfully my taste for scotch is not as limited as my page count on the topic. My advice, as ever, is to find what's right for you through exploration, experimentation and—if you truly hate the taste of something—expectoration. Just don't take a huge sip if you're skittish. Save the good stuff for the rest of us.

The Five Scotch Production Regions...

Speyside

Roughly 50% of the world's scotch distilleries are in Speyside. The sheer number of producers means there's a great variety in flavor among Speysides, but generally they can be described as light and grassy with hints of apple, nutmeg and vanilla. They usually exhibit some smoky and complex flavors as well.
GLENFIDDICH 12 YEAR Sweet notes of pear develop into creamy butterscotch and latent oak.

Highlands

The Highlands is the largest region by landmass and boasts almost 30 distilleries. Given the amount of geographical differences, the whiskies produced here have a broad range. Because of their proximity to the ocean, coastal offerings are a little saltier overall, but generally, Highlands offer notable peat smokiness with hints of heather and honey in drier offerings.
HIGHLAND PARK 18 YEAR Named Best Spirit in the World from noted spirits writer F. Paul Pacult, it features mouthwatering acidity, sweet smoke and brine with notes of honey and salt.

Lowlands

The southernmost part of Scotland has only three distilleries (the "Lowland Ladies," Glenkinchie, Bladnoch and Auchentoshan). Famously triple distilled for a lighter style, most are floral and fruity with notes of grass and honeysuckle underscored by hints of toffee and cinnamon.
AUCHENTOSHAN 12 YEAR A subtle offering with smooth notes of burnt cream, citrus and almonds with green tea.

Islay

This island is only nine miles in length but is home to nine different distilleries. Because of heavy rainfall and constant sea spray, the peat on the island is particularly pungent. Drying the barley over peat fires imparts a bold flavor of smoke combined with salt and seaweed. As such, Islay whiskies are not for the faint of heart. I think the negative associations people attach to Scotch arises from drinking Islay scotches before they knew what they were in for. Oh well—more for me.
LAPHROAIG 10 YEAR Bold peat smoke, seawater, kelp and iodine. Like a campfire on the beach in the rain.

Campbeltown

With only three distilleries still in operation, this west coast town produces some of the most distinctive whiskies available. Because of its location, it gains the peaty and salty flavors of an Islay but still maintains a fruity balance of toffee and vanilla. It also has an added aroma of damp wool that helps give the spirit a distinctive marker.
SPRINGBANK 10 YEAR Citrus and pear with notes of smoke followed by cinnamon and vanilla with a salty finish.

THE **Thrust and Parry**
with the Debonair

Gary "Gaz" Regan is considered by many (myself included) to be a master in the world of cocktails and mixology. He's written numerous books on the subject, tended more bars than most people will visit in their lifetimes and has been a mentor and teacher to many of the finest bartenders of our era. He's also created several cocktails that have made their way into the popular canon, including the Debonair, a thoughtful riff on the Whiskey Mac. "In the 1990s I was asked to present a segment on single malts on the Food Network, and I chose to feature single malt cocktails live on air," recalls Regan. "Back then nobody—and I do mean nobody—used single malts in cocktails, and my feature piece raised many an eyebrow among the hierarchy of the Manhattan food world."

One of those drinks, the Debonair ("A name I confess to finding by consulting a thesaurus," notes Regan) is a simple mixture of single malt and Domaine de Canton ginger liqueur, finished with a lemon twist as an aromatic garnish. Manhattan's upper crust might have scoffed at the idea, but the cocktail took off despite (or perhaps because of) its bucking of foodie sensibilities. "The Debonair made its way onto the cocktail list at New York's Rainbow Room, where my friend, Dale Degroff (pg. 38)—then the head bartender there—told me they sold enough of that one cocktail to polish off a whole case of scotch every month," says Regan. "Not too shabby."

Though the Debonair still surfaces from time to time on cocktail menus all over the world, its creator agrees it's due for a bit of an upgrade. Enter the Thrust and Parry, another of Gaz's contributions to the cocktail canon. "There have been incredible changes in the world of mixed drinks since the Debonair was introduced, and although I believe that the quaff still holds up, I've learned enough, I hope, in the last decade or so to dismember the drink and reassemble it in a slightly more intricate manner," says Regan. "I chose to use the 12-year-old Highland Park scotch as the base, and I've added a couple of new ingredients, seeking a more intricate drink than its forebear. The Canton ginger liqueur is staying put, though—it's a delightful dram that loves to thrust and parry with a damned good scotch." No thesarus needed to name this one, I suppose.

I concur. I'm also a big fan of Gaz's decision to add another punch of smoke via the mezcal rinse, a clever addition that increases the drink's overall aroma and savory flavor. If you have one, I recommend putting the mezcal in an atomizer and spraying the inside of the chilled glass with it to intensify the aroma further.

THE THRUST AND PARRY

.25 oz Del Maguey Vida Mezcal, as a rinse

.75 oz Domaine de Canton ginger liqueur

2 oz Highland Park 12-year-old single malt scotch

3 small pieces of candied ginger on a cocktail skewer, for garnish

Combine the first two ingredients over ice and stir to chill. Coat the inside of a chilled glass with the mezcal as a rinse. Pour in a Nick and Nora glass.

Garnish with candied ginger.

DEBONAIR

1 oz Domaine de Canton ginger liqueur

2.5 oz Oban or Springbank single malt scotch

Stir over ice and strain into a chilled Cocktail glass.

Garnish with lemon twist.

THE **Blue Blazer**

Classic **COCKTAIL**

Jerry "The Professor" Thomas was at the height of his bartending career in New York in the mid 1800s. In an effort to both delight his guests as well as serve them a delicious cocktail, he created the Blue Blazer. Mixing it is a show-stopping display of pyrotechnic finesse that results in a superlative hot toddy (fun fact: the toddy is named after the water it contains, referred to as such because it was drawn from Tod's Well, Edinburgh's largest water supplier). It also creates a legitimate threat to your surroundings (and clothing) in a way most cocktails can only do through supreme overconsumption. Carefully pouring the flaming liquid from one mug to the other repeatedly to heat the drink is a beautiful sight to behold, but it requires both preparation and practice to properly execute. If "patient" and "diligent" and "extremely careful" aren't words people normally associate with you, consider the fire-free version.

.5 oz demerara syrup (or honey)

3 oz boiling water

4 oz cask strength scotch

SPECIAL EQUIPMENT

2 metal pint sized mugs with a flared lip

Long match or stick lighter

Tea cups or coffee mugs

The recipe makes two drinks, as all this work should yield more than one drink.

First, bring down the lights to increase visibility. In one mug, add the sweetener, scotch and half of the boiling water. Tilt the mug on an angle and, using a long match or stick lighter, carefully ignite the scotch. Gently pour half the contents into the second mug. Carefully pour it back into the first mug stretching the mugs apart so the flaming liquid travels farther. Repeat a few times to the delight of your onlookers. Using the bottom of one mug, smother the flames by placing it on top of the other mug. Once extinguished, pour half the contents into each serving vessel. Top up with remaining boiling water.

Garnish with a lemon twist.

FLAME ON (OR OFF)

It should go without saying that both safety and preparedness are the watchwords when it comes to adding the dangers of alcohol to the mysteries of fire. But, it doesn't, so I'm saying it here. Make sure you're using flames on a non-flammable surface, and be aware of other potentially flammable agents in the area. To solve both of these problems, I typically work over a sheet pan with a thin layer of water on it. Further, when building drinks of this pyrotechnic nature, it's best to refrain from having them. If you want to be the star of the show, you can't be part of the audience.

When fire and alcohol are paired together, it's typically more about flair or fanfare than the taste of the final product. Take for example the flaming lime shell in the center of a Scorpion Bowl. Though eye catching, it serves more as garnish than flavor agent. In most cases you can omit the flames altogether and simply warm your cocktails by heating the non-alcoholic components in a small pot and adding them to the alcohol in the serving vessel. If you're serving several, consider using a slow cooker as a de facto hot punch bowl.

My Old Piano

A longtime favorite at Amor y Amargo, this drink was created by my dear friend and a real mensch, Mr. Ari Form. Rye is the drink's backbone, with a subtly smoky hit from the mezcal and savory finish provided by the Kümmel, a coriander, cumin and fennel seed liqueur. The bitters lighten the aroma with the florality of apple blossoms while vermouth lends a rich mouthfeel. Ari was convinced this was how his family's old piano smelled and likely tasted. Either way, it's beautiful music.

2 dashes apple bitters

.25 oz Kümmel

.5 oz mezcal

.75 oz Carpano Antica

1.5 oz rye

Stir over ice and serve up in an Old Fashioned glass.

No garnish.

SAVOR THE SAVORY

As a former chef and current bartender, I often say "I used to cook food; now I just make chilled soup." This is truly how I approach my drink making process. And given that I worked in the world of appetizing food for so long, that's why I'm particularly drawn to the more savory recipes in the cocktail canon. I'm much quicker to grab a bottle of Kümmel (coriander, cumin and fennel seed liqueur) than I am to reach for, say, cranberry juice. Given that we're only equipped to perceive five flavors, three of which lean toward savory, there's plenty of room for making great cocktails with savory components (classics like the Manhattan, Gibson or Bloody Mary come to mind). Plus, culinary arts are finding their way behind bars everywhere— as well they should. Chefs are practiced at the craft of tasting and understanding flavor combinations in food, a skill that easily translates to liquids as well. Smoked cocktails, housemade pickles and shrubs, and even boozy marshmallows are making appearances on menus all over largely due to chefs in the kitchen or chef-minded bartenders flexing their muscles in a different way. So embrace the savory—you won't look back.

Pumpernickel

7 dashes (yup, 7) Angostura bitters

.5 oz Punt e Mes

.75 oz Amaro Abano

1.5 oz 100° rye whiskey

Stir with plenty of ice to chill and dilute. Strain into a chilled glass.

Lemon twist, discarded.

Sother Says
If you find this drink to be a little too spicy, you can back off some of the Angostura to taste. But why would you hurt me like that?

What can I say, Mr. Form (pg. 86) loves his rye whiskey. Plus, he's such an agreeable person to be around, he inspires people to create drinks. Ari would often pour us mid shift shots of rye whiskey with 14 dashes (not a typo) of Angostura bitters to fortify us for the rest of a busy night. I enjoyed them so much I extrapolated the shot into a cocktail. Amaro Abano has a full aroma of white pepper with dried fruit and the heavy dose of bitters pushes all that spice forward. Dark, spicy and rye, just like pumpernickel. Now all I need is a schmear.

Ranch Hand

It's no secret that when it comes to Jägermeister, the extremely polarizing bitter herbal liqueur from Germany, I'm firmly in the "I love it" camp. It's loaded with star anise, ginger and grapefruit with an appealing texture. I often sneak it into cocktails as a secret weapon and flavor bomb. Last summer, I was working an event at a desert resort and wanted to offer partygoers an alternative to all the juicy drinks they'd have during the daily pool parties. This is effectively another in the myriad Old Fashioned variations. Sarsaparilla syrup adds more anise as well as some menthol and a little sassafras to the mix. You can build this in advance and have it ready to pour for service, but it's also delicious served long on ice and topped with seltzer.

1.5 oz rye

.5 oz Jägermeister

Sarsaparilla syrup (pg 245)

Pour the rye and Jägermeister into a 6-oz glass bottle or flask. Top with sarsaparilla to fill. Seal and chill in the refrigerator overnight. Crack 'em open when you're ready to serve.

Alternatively, you can serve the two spirits as a highball topped with your favorite root beer.

No garnish.

Southern Baptist

I'm a big fan of highballs for their simplicity. However, unless I'm sticking to just seltzer and spirit, I'm often disappointed by them. It's not the spirits that let me down but the sodas, which leaves me with two options: skipping them altogether or complicating what should have been simple; I choose the latter. Here, I'm riffing on the Presbyterian, a whiskey and ginger ale highball, but this version is shaken and served up. For my money, ginger ale can't hold a candle to fresh ginger syrup. If you've got no way to juice ginger at home, seek out your local juice bar and have them do the work for you. Augment your final syrup with an ounce of rye whiskey per 16 oz of syrup to give it more shelf stability so you can make enough for it to be worth your time. The resulting bright and sharp cocktail is reminiscent of a zesty daiquiri. If you're missing the bubbles, serve it long on ice and top with seltzer. Amen.

.75 oz fresh lime juice

.75 oz ginger syrup (pg 244)

2 oz rye

Combine all ingredients in a shaker. Then add ice. Shake vigorously and double strain into a Cocktail glass.

Garnish with candied ginger.

Old Pal

The Old Pal is an established classic in its own right, but it's a variation on the iconic Negroni (pg. 37)—inside my top three all time favorite cocktails. It could also be considered an augmented Manhattan (pg 74), another of my top three favorites, so it's easy to see why I enjoy this cocktail so much. My ratio is a bit skewed from the equal parts classic to allow the spirit to stand forward a little more. Plus, dry vermouth stands in for the sweet, giving the drink a thinner, drier mouthfeel. The result is a citrus-scented, slightly bitter and very austere drink. I reach for a Negroni in summer and a Manhattan in winter—the Old Pal takes the stage in both spring and fall.

.75 oz dry vermouth

.75 oz Campari

1.5 oz rye

Stir with ice, strain into chilled cocktail glass.

Lemon twist, discarded.

Sother Says
Swap out the dry vermouth for sweet and bourbon for rye and you've got yourself a Boulevardier.

Hambone

I like the surprise and challenge of blending together things that may not seem compatible at first. As an example, most people might not think to pair the spiciness of rye whiskey with the rich sweetness of pineapple juice, but I love it. Coupled with the spice and citrus flavor of cardamom and the silky texture of pineapple juice, this whiskey cocktail will have you slapping out a beat in no time. Plus, pineapple juice naturally foams up when shaken and creates a beautiful head that can be decorated or "painted" with bitters (inset). Pineapple juice is also a great candidate for smoking to really turn up the savory nature of drinks like this one.

1 green cardamom pod

.25 oz heavy cinnamon clove syrup (pg 244)

.5 oz pineapple juice

.5 oz lemon juice

1 oz Wild Turkey Rye

Muddle the green cardamom pod with the syrup. Add remaining ingredients and ice, shake and double strain into a cocktail glass.

Garnish with drops of Angostura bitters.

HOW TO PAINT WITH BITTERS

As I've written before, aroma makes up 90% of flavor. For this reason, I often use bitters to decorate or "paint" the top of my drinks, particularly if they've got a little foam on top from a frothy juice or egg white. That final burst of aromatic compounds just as you take a sip will really alter the flavor of the drink. But it also looks cool. I like to create a sno-cone effect on the Rough Seas by splashing the bitters on the crushed ice with a haphazard style. On especially foamy drinks I am a bit more precise. Just let the head of a foamy drink like the Hambone settle and, using the dropper from a bottle of bitters, make dots on top of the drink. Then, gently drag a toothpick through them to create little heart shapes. Or, draw straight lines and leave them stark. You can do this. Make Bob Ross proud.

Rye Cappuccino

There's something about mixing coffee with alcohol that just seems right. The Rye Cappuccino is a perfect punctuation mark to a great evening among friends, or a boozy treat to start your day. Caffeinated and high octane, I created this cocktail for my friend Todd who commonly had a shot of espresso laced with whiskey in preparation for a big night out.

The technique of whip shaking cream flavored with bitters and using it as a float on top of a cocktail is extremely maliable. I'm constantly using it to create an added layer of flavor and eye appeal to drinks of all manner, so feel free to apply the technique to any drinks with cream.

2 dashes chocolate bitters

1 oz cold espresso

.5 oz brown sugar syrup (pg 244)

2 oz rye

.75 oz heavy cream

Shake first 3 ingredients and strain into a chilled Cordial glass. Shake cream and bitters in a tin without ice to whip. Float cream on top.

Garnish with dark chocolate espresso beans.

MAKE YOUR OWN CORDIALS

Cordials or liqueurs are sweetened infusions that can be sipped on their own, typically after a meal as a liquid dessert, or used to modify cocktails. They can be made from fruits, nuts, dairy or spices, and there are hundreds of them commercially available. But where's the joy in purchasing something you can make pretty easily and relatively consistently (unlike bitters) on your own?

The process is pretty straightforward: Choose a spirit that matches your desired usage outcome, then add your flavor agent and sweetener. Allow to steep for several days to weeks then strain and use. You should use a neutral spirit like vodka or white rum coupled with a fruit of your choice and plain sugar for your first outing. This will give you an idea of ratios

you might like and will give you confidence to try trickier combinations. I make a rye and coffee cordial (which the Rye Cappuccino is a bit of a riff on) using espresso beans, demerara sugar and orange twists, but the sky's the limit. Dark rum and bananas sweetened with maple syrup and cinnamon? Sounds like breakfast to me! My rye cordial recipe on page 246.

GUEST BARTENDER **RYAN MAYBEE**

Pendergast #2

"This cocktail is inspired by 'Boss Tom' Pendergast, the businessman who 'ran' Kansas City during Prohibition, and kept things swinging. He's largely credited with making KC the biggest party town in the country during that time, which led to the rise of it as a Jazz town and to the invention of bebop."

That's Ryan Maybee, a renaissance man in my field, talking about his cocktail, Pendergast #2. He's an accomplished bartender, bar owner and, now, distiller of spirits and maker of amaro. Plus he's tall, well spoken and good looking—it borders on unfair. He planted his flag firmly in Kansas City, Missouri, the "Paris of the Plains," and if you find yourself in that part of the world you'd be doing yourself a disservice by not visiting his establishments, the Rieger Hotel Grill & Exchange, as well as its subterranean speakeasy-inspired bar Manifesto.

The coolest thing about Ryan's cocktail is it includes his personal hooch in the form of J. Rieger's Kansas City Whiskey. The method for Kansas City style, wherein a distiller would add a small percentage of sherry to the finished product, was lost to Prohibition but uncovered by Ryan and is now its own designation. The whiskey has a nutty-sweet finish and those notes, coupled with sweet vermouth and herbal Benedictine, offer the structure of a classic like the Vieux Carre (pg 214). I also appreciate that this cocktail is meant to be served "down," as that's how it would've likely been presented during Prohibition when drinks weren't served in a lot of fancy glassware. Boss Tom would approve.

3–4 dashes orange bitters

.5 oz Bénédictine

.75 oz sweet vermouth

.5 oz J. Rieger's Kansas City Whiskey

Combine all ingredients in mixing glass with ice and stir until well-chilled. Strain, down, into a chilled Rocks glass, sans ice.

Garnish with lemon zest.

Sother Says
If you'd prefer, you can garnish this drink with a lemon twist as opposed to zest, as I've done.

Rye-Tai

Variations on classic drinks can find their inspiration anywhere. In this case, an easy play on words and two simple substitutions create a completely new drink—one with its own personality and distinctive charm. The classic Mai Tai finds its strength in Jamaican rum with notes of orange peel, vanilla, coffee and even ginger. This version uses spicy, 100-proof Rittenhouse Rye boasting flavors of orange, black pepper, cinnamon and wood. There are easy comparisons here: Pepper and cinnamon notes in the rye are warm and spicy like the vanilla and ginger back notes of Jamaican rum. Old Overholt Rye also has a dryness associated with the flavor of peanuts or peanut shells that pairs well with nutty orgeat. That syrup, combined with lemon juice and Cointreau, is reminiscent of a rich lemonade, and if you haven't tried American whiskey in lemonade, well, you haven't lived well enough. Needless to say, the resulting amalgam is a curious but delicious homage to the classic with a decidedly Southern bent—like an island drink, but on the Outer Banks.

1 oz fresh lime juice

.5 oz orgeat (pg 246)

.5 oz Cointreau

1 oz Rittenhouse Rye

1 oz Old Overholt Rye

Whip shake and pour over crushed ice in a double Old Fashioned glass.

Garnish with lime shell. NOTE: For maximum aromatic impact, serve the lime shell with the skin side out.

Yellow Mellow

Mellow Corn is a straight corn whiskey, meaning its mashbill must have at least 80% corn. Additionally, it's aged for four years in used Heaven Hill barrels. The nose has layers of corn, vanilla and dried banana. I was in search of a cocktail that was unconventional in its pairing while keeping the balance of whimsy to drinkability proportional. Pineapple and corn whiskey seemed a likely candidate. I often think of a Venn diagram when creating drinks. Pineapple and ginger are complementary, while ginger and whiskey are a classic pairing, so I knew these flavors would all meet up in the center. Shrubs are such a fun and semi-clever way to add acidity into cocktails, and this one is bright and easy to make. The seltzer keeps it light. Sip it up and mellow out.

2 oz Mellow Corn Whiskey

1 oz pineapple ginger shrub (pg 245)

Seltzer

Shake first two ingredients vigorously with plenty of ice. Strain into a Highball glass of ice and top with seltzer.

No garnish.

New Boots

I was invited to a backyard barbecue at my friend (and fellow southerner) Todd's house in Brooklyn last summer. I didn't have the time to prepare a dish for the table so instead I brought a liter bottle of this cocktail to share with all the guests. It was such a hit I eventually put it on the menu at the bar. It's basically an augmented Old Fashioned. Bourbon mixed with the cola flavors of the CioCiaro is a natural fit. The addition of cherry bark vanilla bitters moves it to an almost nostalgic Cherry Coke flavor. Then it takes a savory turn with the addition of the BBQ bitters. Sure, the notion of this drink might not have occurred to a greenhorn, but this ain't my first rodeo. (Or so you might say after you have one or three of these....)

1 dash Bitter End Memphis Barbecue Bitters

1 dash Bittercube Cherry Bark Vanilla Bitters

1 oz Amaro CioCiaro

1 oz bourbon

Build in an Old Fashioned glass. Add one large ice cube. Stir to combine.

Garnish with an orange twist.

Char №. 8

Bourbon, by law, must be aged in a newly charred barrel, and the level of char is numbered based on length of time over the flame. A 35 second char, or No. 3, is most common. The research team at the highly awarded Buffalo Trace distillery did an experimental run of barrels to No. 7, but no one has gone further than that. My goal was to build a balanced cocktail that had layers of smoke as a more direct tie to the idea of charring. The additional smokiness in this cocktail comes from the peated whisky with an extra layer of broody dark "char" coming from the amaro. Zucca is made with Chinese rhubarb which, when dried, has a naturally smoky flavor. Plus, the dark color of the liquid lends itself the look of something that's been burnt. Jerry Thomas decanter bitters have a dried fruit and sherry flavor that helps all these bold flavors to mingle. The resulting full-bodied drink tastes smokey and charred well beyond the typical No. 3.

2 dashes Bitter Truth Jerry Thomas' Own Decanter Bitters

.25 oz Zucca Rubarbaro

.25 oz Compass Box Peat Monster Scotch

1.5 oz bourbon

Build in an Old Fashioned glass. Add one large ice cube. Stir to combine.

No garnish.

THE Seelbach

Named after the stately hotel in downtown Louisville, KY (fun fact: in *The Great Gatsby*, Daisy and Tom are described as having spent their wedding night here. So did my editor!), the Seelbach cocktail holds the unique distinction of having two genesis stories that will likely both live forever. Back in 1995, when Adam Seger ran the bar program there, he put the hotel's "signature drink" on the menu after claiming to have discovered its charming origin: in 1912 a honeymooning couple (not Tom and Daisy, nor my editor) were staying at the hotel. One fateful evening at the bar the gentleman ordered his bride a glass of champagne and a Manhattan for himself. The bartender accidentally spilled the champagne into the Manhattan. He quickly remade the order for his guests but later sipped the clumsy concoction, and from there the idea for the signature drink of the hotel was formed. Romantic, yes. Plausible, yes. True? Nope.

In 2016, Seger stepped forward to unburden himself of the story he'd perpetrated on the public and revealed that just like the cocktail, he'd created its history from his own imagination. Over those two decades, the story had been repeated in numerous press outlets as well as printed in notable cocktail books written by luminaries in the field. This, I believe, is going to stand the test of time as the drink's second origin story. Interesting history or not, the drink has merit. It's got a good balance of bitter to sweet, much like an Old Fashioned. Plus cocktail historian David Wondrich (one of the few in the field who never wrote about the cocktail as he couldn't verify the story) says any drink can be made better with the addition of champagne, and I tend to agree with him. Even though the original story has been debunked, now there are two stories to tell. And for me, storytelling is the best part of bartending anyway.

---

7 dashes Angostura bitters

7 dashes Peychaud's Bitters

.5 oz triple sec

1 oz bourbon, preferably Old Forester

5 oz domestic Brut sparkling wine, preferably Korbel Brut, chilled

In a mixing glass three-quarters filled with ice, combine first 4 ingredients. Stir until chilled, about 30 seconds.

Strain the mixture into a Champagne flute. Top with the sparkling wine.

Garnish with orange twist.

Sother Says
In the event you create a cocktail you love, name it, post it on social media and watch it take the world by storm. Or, discover to your horror that it's existed for decades. Just don't keep it to yourself.

Bain's Existence
with Pendennis Club

The Pendennis Club cocktail is made with gin, apricot liqueur and lemon juice, and unlike the Seelbach cocktail (also hailing from Louisville, KY) it was definitely not made up by a bartender 20 years ago. It's a classic, albeit a stuffy one, and I felt it needed a bit of an upgrade. I named this riff on the Pendennis Club after the establishment's most famous headwaiter, Henry Bain, who created their famous Bain Sauce sometime during his 40-year tenure there. I imagine Mr. Bain overheard plenty of gossip and witnessed many spectacles during his time at the Pendennis, all the while holding his tongue. I like to think after a long day serving Louisville's elite good ol' boys, he'd enjoy this cocktail, a smooth concoction of apricot-laced bourbon sweetened with lemon oil syrup, also known as oleo saccahrum. The drink's success really hinges on the oleo saccahrum, but it's a wild card that you can easily master (recipe on pg 245). Once you do, there's no end in sight to the variations that can be made to the basic template. For the garnish I've chosen macerated apricots, which may be the easiest thing in this book to replicate: in a shallow bowl, barely cover some dried apricots in equal parts water and bourbon. They'll plump right up.

BAIN'S EXISTENCE

2 dashes Peychaud's Bitters

.75 oz lemon oleo saccharum (pg 245)

.75 oz Rothman & Winter Orchard Apricot

2 oz bourbon

Shake all ingredients together with ice. Strain into a double Old Fashioned glass with ice.

Garnish with macerated apricot.

PENDENNIS CLUB

Classic COCKTAIL

2 dashes Peychaud's Bitters

.5 oz lime juice

1 oz Rothman & Winter Orchard Apricot

2 oz Plymouth gin

Shake all ingredients together with ice. Strain into a double Old Fashioned glass with ice.

Garnish with a lemon twist or cherry.

HOW TO FEEL OUT A BAR

A simple guide to getting where you want to drink.

A bar is a bar is a bar is simply no longer apt. First, there are "diners," bars that serve a wide variety of drinks in a nondescript atmosphere. Most of the drinks tend to be poorly executed by a staff of clock punchers. That doesn't mean you can't enjoy yourself at one, but if the space itself looks like it's franchised, chances are their beverage program is going to be cookie cutter and cluttered and underwhelming overall.

Then there are more specialized spots that serve better quality items with a staff that's more drink savvy, but they still offer things they probably shouldn't in an effort to please a wider audience. Yes, you can get a frozen piña colada in Cleveland. But it likely won't be as good as what you find in the Florida Keys.

Then there are venues with a more focused approach. Sure, you can order a cocktail at a wine bar, and they'll likely come through with something you enjoy. But it's a bit like ordering pasta at a sushi bar. They may have it, but that's not what you came for.

All this is to say, if four friends said to themselves "Let's get dinner," they wouldn't head to the nearest place that serves food. First they'd discuss what everyone wants and come to a consensus. This way, even if one of them wanted tacos but the group decided on Korean fare they'd at least know what they were in for before entering the door.

Conversely, if those four same friends say "Let's get a drink," they typically end up at the nearest bar without forming a consensus, meaning that if one wanted fine wine, one fine cocktails, one beers and shots and one tiki drinks, odds are all four friends (and possibly the staff) will be disappointed.

Gone are the days when every bar carried everything. This is a positive move, but it requires a little planning on your part as a guest. You'll generally have a better time if you know what you want and where to find it.

Often, the onus is on the guest to suss out what type of bar they've wandered into. Take 30 seconds to examine your environment, and I guarantee you'll have a better experience. If you notice they don't have jiggers on the bar, then it's probably best to forgo multi-ingredient cocktails. Similarly, if you see unrefrigerated vermouth on the back-bar with a speed pour on it, you might shy away from ordering a Manhattan. No sign of a cocktail menu? Probably best to order a beer. And if the floor is sticky, you may want to stick to bottled beer—if they can't keep the bar in good order, they probably aren't cleaning those beer lines too often. Look down the bar and see what type of drinks the crowd has and follow suit. I don't order shots of Jägermeister at a known cocktail den, just as I don't order a New York sour at my local dive.

Kentucky Buck

Erick Castro is a dynamo or possibly a whirling dervish. Charming and quick-witted, he's done it all. Former brand ambassador for Beefeater Gin, bartender, bar owner and creator and star of the popular *Bartender at Large* documentary and podcast, I question if he ever sleeps. On top of all that he still finds time to create incredible cocktails, one of which—not unlike Erick himself—has become something of a global phenomenon: the Kentucky Buck.

Bucks are a classification of cocktails that are comprised of a spirit, citrus juice and ginger beer or ale, the most famous of which is the Moscow Mule (pg. 21). And Erick bests it. "Around the time I came up with it I was really into *The Gentleman's Companion* by Charles H. Baker Jr. (a must read!), and I noticed that the Buck was a popular drink during that period (the '20s and '30s)," says Erick. "But I never saw it made with American whiskey. It typically appeared with rum or scotch or gin. And that seemed strange to me. So knowing ginger goes really well with bourbon, but also wanting to give it a San Francisco twist, we made it with strawberries."

Using seasonal strawberries from a farm just outside the city, the Kentucky Buck made its debut on Bourbon & Branch's 2008 spring menu. But it wasn't until Erick put it on the regular menu at the Rickhouse, one of Bourbon and Branch's sister restaurants, that it really started to take off. "It became a beast. We were selling 700 a week at the beginning." The Kentucky Buck has since been named by *Imbibe Magazine* as one of its "Modern Classics." One sip and it's easy to see why. The final product is snappy, with bright hits of ginger tamed by what's essentially strawberry lemonade and added notes of spice from the Angostura bitters.

Being a long drink, I make mine with an overproof bourbon like Wild Turkey to cut through to the front of the line. Among the drink's further attributes is its ability to take a beating. "You can make it wrong, but it still tastes good. You can use different bitters or lime instead of lemon—the wiggle room on it is so wide that no matter what you do to it, it's still going to turn out OK," says Erick, likening the recipe to that of a margarita. "It's dummy proof."

---

2 dashes Angostura bitters

.5 oz simple syrup

.75 oz lemon juice

1 medium strawberry

2 oz bourbon

Ginger beer

Add all ingredients except the ginger beer to shaker. Shake and double strain through a mesh strainer into a Collins glass filled with fresh ice. Top with ginger beer.

Garnish with a lemon wheel and strawberry.

Sagebrush Swizzle

Fresh sage leaves

.75 oz tart cherry syrup (pg 244)

1 oz lemon juice

2 oz rye

Cherry bitters

Using a muddler, press sage leaves into the bottom of a Collins glass to express their oil. Loosely fill the glass with pebble ice. Pour the syrup, juice and rye into a shaker with 10–12 pieces of pebble ice. Shake vigorously to aerate and chill. Pour into prepared glass. Swizzle the mixture using a swizzle stick (or your bar spoon, if you must) until the glass is frosty. Fill with more pebble ice, forming a dome on top. Heavily dash with bitters.

Garnish with sage leaf and cherry.

When I'm at a bar trying to decide what to drink and I see a swizzle go past, the agony is immediately over as my choice has been made for me. I love them. And after practicing the techniques required to make a swizzle, you'll quickly see that they're almost as fun to make as they are to imbibe. This version is a riff on the template, swapping out rye and replacing the usual falernum with a homemade cherry syrup. It's essentially a sweet-tart cherry lemonade punched up with American whiskey. The sage leaves bring in an herbal quality, plus a bit of dryness on the tongue.

A WORD ABOUT SWIZZLES

Though I carry the reputation of being the "bitter guy," it's no secret I'm a sucker for a swizzle. They hail from the Caribbean and most people agree Bermuda is the country of origin, while The Swizzle Inn on Bailey's Bay serves the region's best. It's a tall rum drink on pebble ice that's whipped to a frosty froth using the stem of the Quararibea turbinata, or swizzle stick plant, spun between the palms like a Boy Scout trying to make a fire. Traditional swizzles are made from tropical fruits and rum sweetened with falernum, a syrup flavored with island spices and citrus and can be made with or without alcohol. I recommend making your own using lime and grapefruit peels, allspice berries, fresh ginger and cane sugar. Augment the syrup with one ounce of overproof rum per quart to lend some shelf stability. It's an integral component of many drinks, including the classic rum swizzle. There's no greater joy than enjoying one beachside on an island. Or at your local. Or in your basement. Honestly, I'll drink one anywhere.

Bourbon Hot Chocolate

2 Tbsp Sother's Cocoa Mix

3 oz hot milk

2 oz Wild Turkey 101 bourbon

Combine all ingredients in a mug and enjoy!

Top with marshmallows.

Nothing says winter warmer quite like a cup of hot chocolate. And it's even better when made from scratch (and with bourbon to boot)! My recipe includes a little touch of heat from chili powder that serves to excite the palate, so don't skip it. There's also powdered milk in the mix to create a richer body, but I still recommend making it with whole milk instead of skim or water.

Plus, if you've never made your own marshmallows, now is the time. You'll never go back to Stay Puft again.

MAKE YOUR OWN BOOZY MARSHMALLOWS

Marshmallows are delicious, decidedly more so when made with booze. And even though making them involves some specific techniques, they're relatively easy to produce. No one is going to be dissatisfied with a bourbon hot cocoa if marshmallows aren't offered, but everyone will be shocked by your culinary skills if you made them yourself—especially if you made them with Chartreuse! Chartreuse is the herbal liqueur for which the color was named, and it's been produced by Carthusian monks since 1737 from a 1605 recipe. The closely guarded recipe featuring more than 130 botanicals is known only by two monks at any given time. The secret will likely never get out, as they also operate under a vow of silence. The tight-lipped bunch started making it as an herbal remedy to cure ails, and it packs quite a punch. At 110 proof, a little goes a long way. The marshmallows will add an herbal quality to the cocoa that'll make you feel like you're on an Alpine mountainside after a day on the slopes. Recipe on page 246.

Blackberry Buck

Bucks, like mules, are mixed drinks that involve ginger beer and juice. My Blackberry Buck uses blackberries as well as spicy ginger syrup plus the addition of balsamic vinegar to heighten the kick, as it were. This cocktail takes the Buck and amplifies its highlights by adding some savory components including balsamic vinegar and fresh pepper. The vinegar serves to add to the tartness and acidity of the lemon juice as well as play up the snap of ginger but, as its been aged in barrels, there's also an interesting interplay with the whiskey. Fresh cracked pepper on top adds to the aroma as you bring the drink to your lips for each sip. Typically, I reach for lighter vinegars to incorporate into cocktails but this one has enough backbone to handle the depth of flavor of a darker vinegar.

Adding vinegars to cocktails gives them a boost of extra acidity as well as a deeper more complex flavor. This technique is nothing new: drinking vinegars and shrubs have been around for ages. In the southeastern United States, it's common to dash the brine from sport peppers into a beer. Plus, the Pickle Back (a shot of whiskey followed by a shot of pickle brine) was popularized in Brooklyn in 2006 At The Bushwick Country Club. A favorite watering hole of mine at that time. I even had a hand in helping them fix the recipe for their frozen bourbon and coke and it's still on the menu today!

2 blackberries

.75 oz lemon juice

.25 oz ginger syrup

.25 oz balsamic vinegar

2 oz bourbon

Ginger beer

2 cracks fresh ground pepper

Muddle blackberries in a tin and shake next 5 ingredients with plenty of ice. Strain into a highball glass and add fresh ice. Top with ginger beer and pepper.

Garnish with blackberries.

NOTES ON ACIDITY

When making cocktails, one of the goals is to strike a balance among the flavors present. Too much sweetener and you'll have a flabby mouthfeel, too little and the burn from alcohol takes the lead. Acidity is a key factor in your cocktail's drinkability too. It's usually pretty easy to add acidity using citrus juices, but there is a noticeable hurdle when using orange juice. It simply isn't tart enough to stand up for itself in mixed drinks and often needs augmentation from lime juice. Sadly, the amount of lime needed is usually too much and the orange flavor is lost. It's time to mess with Mother Nature! With the addition of some easily obtained "molecular gastronomy" ingredients, you can "acid adjust" juices to be as acidic as lime juice. Just add 32 grams of citric acid powder and 20 grams Malic Acid to every liter of orange juice and shake to dissolve. You can use this ratio to put more acidity into other juices too. Try it with pineapple or apple juice! Now your Blood and Sand is a bright revelation of bullfighting glory instead of a fat steer lumbering around the arena. This method also works quite nicely with fresh pineapple juice.

Jerkwater

This is a whiskey-driven take on the (much more) popular Cosmopolitan. But I prefer this concoction to Carrie and the gals' go-to any day of the week. Hibiscus tea is more tannic and drier than cranberry juice, which helps create a cleaner finish. Whiskey is obviously more assertive than vodka, which helps it stand up to those tannins. And hibiscus tea notwithstanding, it's a little more work-a-day than what you might find in the big city. It's the Cosmo of the Common Man.

.25 oz hibiscus tea syrup (pg 244)

.75 oz lemon juice

1 oz Dry Curaçao (Pierre Ferrand)

1.5 oz American whiskey

Shake and strain into a chilled Nick and Nora glass.

No garnish.

Sother Says

The Cosmo recipe that we all know of today was perfected by Toby Cecchini in New York, and it captured the attention of night lifers all across the Big Apple. The drink was further popularized by its appearance on several episodes of the television series *Sex and the City*.

Salt Peanuts Whiskey

I was asked to prepare a cocktail for an event in New Orleans held at a music venue. I lived in the Crescent City for a few years when I was a younger man, and while there I cultivated a love of live jazz music and Old Fashioneds. The name of this drink is the title of what's now become a jazz standard originally written by Dizzy Gillespie (with the addition of the word whiskey for good measure). In keeping with the name, I feature layers of peanuts incorporated into the components backed up by a few drops of saline solution for extra saltiness. I love using Old Overholt Rye in this cocktail as I have often thought it tasted of peanuts and pencil shavings. The result is a nutty and slightly savory Old Fashioned that'll have you snapping your fingers to the hep beat of the music of life.

Dash roasted peanut infused bitters*

1.5 tsp of roasted peanut syrup*

2 oz Old Overholt Rye

2 drops saline solution*

Build in an Old Fashioned glass. Add large ice cube and gently stir.

Garnish with an orange twist.

*All ingredient recipes can be found on pg 247.

No Mint Julep

The Kentucky Derby is known as "The most exciting two minutes in sports," and it's no secret the Mint Julep is the preferred drink each year on race day. Though I love a good Julep, I often find them to be too sweet—especially if I'm having more than one. A few years ago at Amor y Amargo, we decided to listen to the race on the radio. We assumed the crowd would expect us to make the traditional drink to accompany the horserace, but because we don't use mint at the bar, this was our solution. This version skips the sugar syrup and mint altogether and instead employs Branca Menta. Menta is the second mark from the brand that makes Fernet-Branca. It's sweeter and has a much higher quotient of menthol, and the result is quite bracing. Once built over pebble ice so that it dilutes a bit, this is a delightful cocktail—horse races and over-the-top hats optional.

.5 oz of Branca Menthe

2 oz of 100° bourbon

Combine ingredients over crushed ice.

No garnish.

Good Fences

The Stone Fence was originally made with rum and apple cider and famously had a role in the capture of Fort Ticonderoga during the Revolutionary War. Whiskey eventually became the preferred spirit for the concoction. My version ups the ante by using hard cider rather than fresh pressed. The addition of cinnamon syrup makes for an even more fall-friendly version. Mix up a few of these to enjoy by the fire with your neighbor—provided you have a good fence to hop over when it's time to head home.

.5 oz cinnamon syrup (pg 244)

2 oz bourbon

4 oz hard apple cider

Pour the bourbon and syrup into a Highball glass filled with ice. Top with cider.

Garnish with grated cinnamon and an apple slice.

THE MOST
SENSIBLE
THING TO DO
TO PEOPLE YOU
HATE
IS TO DRINK THEIR
BRANDY

— ELIZABETH TAYLOR

Brandy

'brandē / noun

1. from the Dutch brandewijn; a strong alcoholic spirit distilled from wine or fermented fruit juice

2. a fine girl, or so Looking Glass would have you believe

verb

3. to preserve, flavor or mix with brandy (the spirit, not the girl)

ON BRANDY

One of the oldest categories of spirit still surprises.

It may be a shock to those around me how much I love brandy. I'm pretty reliably drinking whisk(e)y, tequila, rum and, of course, amaro. I sneak brandy in unnoticed.

It's a noble spirit with a dichotomous nature. It's simultaneously regal and common, meaning you can take it seriously or with a grain of salt. Take Cognac, a specific style of brandy named for the region in which it's produced: It has a storied history, the drink of emperors, aged for a lifetime and meant to be sipped from a crystal snifter in a room carved from marble. Alternatively, American apple brandy is made from fruit we wouldn't deem worthy to eat and shot from a glass in a sticky dive bar that's one rogue hair away from a health inspector shutdown. In truth, either brandy could be enjoyed in either setting. In this way, it's a sort of leveler, placing the common man on the same footing as the elite and effete. And while I certainly consider myself a commoner, I too enjoy the unofficial pomp and circumstance involved in casually consuming brandy; the sometimes comically oversized snifter laid sideways in the palm of the hand, gently swirling so the heat of your hand helps coax out the aromas that are then captured in the balloon of the glass; smelling the spirit before sipping, all while engaging in lively conversation. That said, you can have a great conversation after a few shots of the stuff as well. What can I say? Common is as common does.

In keeping with our theme of "everything starts as beer then becomes vodka before morphing into what the maker intends," we've got a slight outlier in the category of brandy. Brandy is made by distilling fermented fruit juice (aka wine) instead. Though grape-based brandies are most typical, all manner of fruits (notably apples, apricots and pears) can be made into brandy—and they are, all over the world. Pomace, the leftover skins, pulp, seeds and stems from pressing juice can also be fermented and made into brandy, referred to as grappa or pomace brandy. The Dutch, pioneers in the art of distillation, first called it Brandewijn meaning "burnt wine." This was because the wine would be heated over a fire, or burned, to distill it.

The wine used to make grape brandy is typically made from early harvest grapes (specifically Ugni-Blanc grapes for Cognac), which have better characteristics for making a distilled spirit. They result in a more acidic wine with a significantly lower sugar content. Wine from these grapes also has a far lower sulphur content than traditional wines. This too is advantageous to the distiller as sulphur reacts with copper to create copper-sulphate, resulting in undesirable flavors and aromas in the final product. Because most brandies are produced using copper pot stills, once again, science saves the day.

Brandy can take on several forms (and as many names) but the process is pretty standard. The base wine is distilled twice. The first run removes most of the water and solids from the wine, and the resulting distillate is called "low wine." Low wine has an ABV of around 30% and typically gets distilled a second time to become un-aged brandy. Overwhelmingly, brandy is produced using copper pot stills as the resulting distillate has more aromatic qualities that harken back to the original fruit. In fact, the use of the column still is forbidden by law in the production of Cognac. However some brandy producers use a column still, the result being a higher yield with a little less character (that's mass production for you). The distillate can then be aged, blended or bottled before going to market. In Cognac, they do all three.

I took a trip to France a few years ago in an effort to both drink and explore Cognac, as well as its older, more mysterious cousin Armagnac (as you may have surmised by now, my vacations often revolve around booze). It was enlightening, adding to the already romanticized notions I held for the category. I suggest doing this in general for any spirit you love. Meeting the makers, seeing their faces and shaking their hands gives you a deeper understanding and appreciation of every sip. I was lucky enough to stroll through vineyards with the growers, tasting grapes along the way as they told me about harvest conditions. I found my way into the barrel-stacked aging rooms, which smelled of old paper and alcohol, like an apothecary's archive had been doused with whiskey. I convinced

the distillers to take me into their "Paradis," a room all Cognac distilleries have, filled with huge glass carboys or "bonbonnes," covered in mold containing their oldest vintages for blending (some from the 1800s!). When I asked about the thick moss-like mold on them, I was informed they act as a security system: as long as the mold is intact, you know no one has disturbed the contents.

For Cognac and Armagnac, the clear liquid coming off the still is then typically aged in oak barrels until it's deemed mature enough to be bottled (in the case of Cognac, the barrels must be built from oak sourced from the Limousin region of France, and the brandy must be aged for a minimum of two years.) When the blender deems it to be matured enough, it's moved from wooden barrels into the glass bonbonnes for storage that won't add anymore flavor. Often these brandies have been in the barrel for decades and, because of a great percentage of loss in both volume and ABV—known as "La part des anges," or "The angels' share"—this brandy is highly concentrated and very useful in small quantities for blending.

Cognac and Armagnac share a similarity with scotch production in that the craft is heavily

"Le Paradis," the room where the oldest brandies are stored, at the Dartigalongue Armagnac Estate in France.

reliant on the skill of a blender, though a few makers choose not to blend their different ages of brandies for bottlings, similar to single malt scotch production. Designations for Cognac and Armagnac mostly depend on age, but because these brandies are typically blended, the grades refer to the youngest spirit in the blend. Many VSOP Cognacs contain liquid far older than the minimum of four years, which helps with consistency of product. VS Cognacs taste of flowers and fresh fruits, while VSOP take on jam-like qualities of dried fruit with hints of vanilla. Toffee and nutty flavors as well as tea notes come with older examples.

Armagnac is the oldest brandy distilled in France and was taken as a therapeutic in the 14th century. Unlike Cognac, which only uses Ugni-Blanc, it's mainly made from three types of grapes: Folle Blanche, Colombard and Baco Blanc. It's produced in a tiny designation in the southwestern region of Gascony. Traditionally, Armagnac is made by using column stills instead of pot stills and distilled only once to achieve an ABV of approximately 52%. It's then aged in oak for a minimum of two years. Water is typically not added prior to bottling.

Younger Armagnac tastes earthy and warm. As they mature, they taste of apricot and quince, with the oldest expressions revealing notes of toffee, coffee, cocoa and caramel. In 2005, the French government granted Armagnac distillers the right to sell Blanche or "white" Armagnac. The brandy equivalent of moonshine, it tastes floral and of green grapes, fig and ginger. I highly recommend trying it if you spot some in the wild.

While we're here talking about the famous brandies of France, I'd be remiss if I didn't mention Pineau des Charentes, created by a happy accident when a Cognac maker inadvertently poured fresh grape juice into what he believed was an empty barrel used to store eau-de-vie (the name given to unaged brandy made from fruit other than grapes). But the barrel wasn't empty. Realizing his error,

Designations for Cognac and Armagnac...

Both Cognac and Armagnac are bottled at no lower than 40% ABV and have official categories as outlined below. The category acronyms, which represent English phrases despite only applying to a French product, were established in the 18th century, when most of the trade was done with the British.

VS
"Very Special," these brandies are aged a minimum of two years.

VSOP
"Very Superior Old Pale," also referred to as Reserve, must be four years old for Cognac, three years for Armagnac.

Napoleon
Named after the diminutive emperor, the brandy with this designation must be at least six years old following rules effective March 2018.

XO
Or "Extra Old," must be at least 10 years old, up from six as of March 2018. It's estimated that these brandies typically include spirits as high as 20 years old in the blend.

Hors d'Âge
Or "Beyond Age" has the same minimum rules as XO, but makers employ this designation when marketing their most high quality blends. In sum: they is fancy.

he put the barrel back into the cellar to ferment, but the alcohol content of the young brandy slowed fermentation. The resulting liquid, essentially an erroneously created fortified wine, was delicious. It's now produced as a side product for many distillers and is largely consumed in France, though a lot makes it out of the country as well. On my previously mentioned trip to France, I was invited into the home of the matriarch of the Royer family, at the time a sixth generation Cognac house. She escorted me to her cellar, where she pulled out a pitcher of Pineau des Charentes for us to enjoy over ice with pastries on the porch. Her late husband had put the barrel in the cellar prior to his passing some 30 years prior. It was delightfully oxidized with flavors of stone fruits and toasted nuts, almost like a softer expression of Vermouth. Pierre Ferrand makes a delicious one at an extremely reasonable price.

In a completely different hemisphere from France, South Africa is producing fine brandies, partly thanks to the arrival of oppressed French Huguenots—also experts in viticulture and oenology—starting in 1691. The rules in this region allow for both column and pot stills to be used, provided the final blend contains no less than 30% potstill brandy. The brandy has to age for a minimum of three years in barrels no larger than 340L (90 gal). It must then be bottled at either 38% or 40% ABV, a strange split that is likely the result of export regulations and taxation.

Designations for South African Brandy...

The practice of brandy production might not be as old as it is in France, but the South Africans, who use Chenin Blanc and Columbard grapes, still have a few established rules determining what a label implies about its contents:

Potstill Brandy
Must be aged at least three years.

Blended Brandy
Is comprised of at least 30% potstill brandy that's been aged for minimum three years. The remainder is blended column still eau de vie.

Vintage Brandy
Is at least 30% potstill brandy aged at least eight years, with the rest comprised of eight-year-aged, column still brandy.

Estate Brandy
Is made at a single estate from start to finish, no matter the still used.

If you're wondering how South Africans can compete with the French for brandy supremacy, you need only know that the South Africans have proven themselves as incredible winemakers year after year, and where there's quality wine, there will eventually be quality brandy. In fact, by 1981, South African brandies were beating French Cognacs in global spirits competitions, and today they consistently create some of the best brandy in the world. KWV and Van Ryns are the names to know.

Another notable brandy style hails from Spain. Brandy de Jerez, made exclusively in its protected designation of origin, the Jerez area of Spain (made up of the three municipalities of Jerez de la Frontera, El Puerto de Santa María and Sanlúcar de Barrameda). A good portion of Brandy de Jerez is used to fortify the famous sherries of the region, but, in their ever-growing knowledge about distilling and more importantly aging brandy, it became just as well regarded as the sherries of the region. It's aged in 500L (132 gallon) American Oak barrels that previously held sherry, and is aged using the traditional solera system (more on pg. 155). As a result of this fractional blending year after year, there are trace amounts of very old brandy in every bottle. Brandy de Jerez's Solera has a minimum average age of six months, Solera Reserva has a minimum average age of one year and Solera Gran Reserva has a minimum average age of three years.

These brandies, like the sherries of the region, can run the gamut from bone dry to syrupy sweet. Typically the younger ones are somewhat drier while older expressions have matured, mellowed and taken on nuances of the barrels over time. Flavors typical to the category in order of age include dry sherry, toasted nuts, ripe fruit, cream, molasses, raisins and burnt caramel. I suggest you explore and find ones you love. They are generally best enjoyed neat, a true classic of the Old World.

Brandies created in the New World may have shorter histories, but they're no less complex. When settlers arrived to the American colonies, they

Barrels of Lepanto Brandy de Jerez being aged using the solera system, at González Byass, a distillery founded in 1835.

brought with them grafts of apple trees that bore fruit that was delicious to eat out of hand. They also saved the seeds from apples they ate on the journey from the Old World. However, due to differing conditions and the fickle nature of apple seeds, they grew into trees that bore extremely bitter, dry fruit not suitable for consumption—so we made cider with them. Starting in the late 18th century, John Chapman championed the proliferation of apples in our burgeoning country. He traveled around teaching the settlers and pioneers how to cultivate these apples, as well as other, more edible varieties. He was a generous man, and was always welcomed into the communities he called on not just because he brought the gift of apple orchard cultivation, but because he was also effectively bringing apple cider. Apple cider begat hard apple cider, which in turn could be distilled or freeze distilled to make apple brandy—all safer to drink than water. John Chapman, aka Johnny Appleseed, was spreading liquid cheer everywhere he went.

Over time, the government realized what a blessing this was and mandated that land grants require the planting of apple orchards to provide citizens with something safe to drink. The making of cider, hard cider and apple brandies was a cottage industry for almost 100 years. But by 1920, when Prohibition became the law of the land, apple orchards all over the country were growing dry, bitter cider apples that no longer had any use. They were routinely chopped down to make space for farming other produce. When Prohibition ended, the country could produce alcohol again, but growing trees of fruit-bearing age took time.

As is often the case when the government makes a terrible decision, there were some holdouts who kept seed stocks and started growing apples again. And thank goodness, because American apple brandy is, frankly, a national treasure. The result of distilling hard cider (and in the case of applejack blending that distillate with neutral grain spirits), American apple brandies typically boast bold flavors of, yes, apple, backed up with hints of baking spice and oak from aging in used whiskey barrels. It's great on its own but also shines in cocktails.

In general, brandy plays well with numerous mixed drink templates, and some of the most beloved classics feature it in some capacity: The Sidecar, the Brandy Alexander (pg 133), the Jack Rose (pg 132), the Vieux Carré (pg 214) and the B&B (that's brandy and Bénédictine, if you've never had the pleasure). Whether you mix, shoot or savor your brandy, I can't stress enough how important it is to try it. A lot of it. As a truly global spirit, its expressions are as varied as the continents themselves. Grab a few bottles and tour the world.

Baked Apple Toddy

Traditional toddies are made with scotch, but I wanted to make something as American as apple pie! This version is basically a fortified mulled cider collaborating on a holiday mixtape with a classic hot toddy. Apple brandy has been a favorite in America ever since our forefathers arrived as settlers and, because of the calendar-based particulars of apple harvest time, it became especially popular around the holidays. It pairs effortlessly with fall ingredients like apple cider and cinnamon, and in this toddy the lemon juice serves to increase the tartness without popping up on its own. The Bar Keep Organic Apple Bitters are bursting with apple blossom aromas that are heightened when served hot, and they help temper the potential sweetness of the drink. Nutmeg and an apple chip complete the picture. Now break out your thermos and let's get Wassailing!

2 dashes Barkeep Organic Apple Bitters

.25 oz lemon juice

.5 oz cinnamon syrup

1 oz hot apple cider

1.5 oz Laird's Apple Brandy

Fill a mug with hot water, letting sit for 1 minute to warm the mug. Pour out the water and add all ingredients.

Garnish with fresh nutmeg and an apple chip.

SOME THOUGHTS ON CIDER

Hard ciders, made by fermenting apple cider (the stuff you're warming up and mulling around the holidays) are often overlooked by the American imbiber, but they're highly consumed in both Europe and Oceania. I suspect this is because many Americans assume cider is too sweet. However, like most categories of alcoholic beverages, they can run the gamut from incredibly dry to sugary sweet. The rules governing the production of hard cider vary from country to country. In the U.S., it ranges from 3.5-12% ABV and must contain a minimum of 50% apple juice. The type of apple juice used is the main factor that determines how the final product will taste. The four recognized categories of cider apples are Sweets, which are low in both tannin and acidity; Sharps, higher acidity and lower tannin; Bittersweets, lower acidity and higher tannin; and Bittersharps, that are high in acid as well as tannin. A skilled cider maker uses all four varieties in concert to achieve a desired result. I tend to prefer drier cider but, as usual, you should taste a lot of them to form your own opinion.

THE Crusta

.5 oz fresh lemon juice

2 dashes Angostura bitters

.5 oz Maraschino liqueur

.5 oz Dry Curaçao

2 oz Cognac

Pare the full peel off a lemon then cut the lemon in half and juice it. Prepare a glass by moistening the rim with lemon and dipping it in sanding/pearl sugar* (if time allows, refrigerate the glass for 20 minutes to create a candied crust), then carefully curl the lemon peel around the inside of the glass. Combine all ingredients in a shaker with ice, stir and strain into glass and add 1 small cube of ice.

   *You can sub in granulated sugar here if you don't have sanding sugar on hand, but there's a definite difference between the two, and I recommend the latter if you can get your hands on it.

Some drinks I like because of the way they taste; others I appreciate because of how important they are to the culture in which I ply my trade. The Crusta is the latter (though it tastes great too). It's significant to both the fundamental basics in cocktail design as well as preparation. I make mine with Cognac, as its fruity nature is enhanced by the orange-based Curaçao and lemon, while Maraschino adds a layer of simultaneous sweetness and dryness (in my early days of creating cocktails, it was my secret weapon). Cinnamon and cardamom notes from the bitters tie all those flavors up with a nice bow. As for preparation, this drink requires a unique, somewhat forgotten lemon peel garnish that defines the drink. Plus, it's the first drink in recorded history that uses sugar as a garnish. If you have the time, sugar the glass in advance and refrigerate it to form a candy-like rim.

THE CRUSTA'S EVOLUTION

Created in New Orleans in the 1850s, the Brandy Crusta is a bit of a category jumper. It closely follows the classic cocktail formula of sugar, water, spirit and bitters but, like a fancy cocktail, takes on the addition of orange liqueur. Then, like a Daisy, it has the addition of lemon juice (albeit a small amount). It further bucks tradition by being a stirred drink even though citrus juice is present, which means it's as closely related to an Old Fashioned as it is to a French 75. It's also the first cocktail to include a sugar-crusted rim (hence its name). It's a vital drink for all these reasons, but for me it's most useful as a bridge cocktail. One of the core tenets of being a hospitable bartender is acting as a spirits concierge for your guests, and the easiest way to teach someone about something new is to relate it to something familiar. The Crusta has enough familiar components that I can describe it as "a brandy Margarita" and use it to coax my guests into the world of brandy. From there it's on to Cognac and Armagnac, opening up a whole new category for them to explore.

Interrobang‽

Cynar is an Amaro that immediately captures the imagination as its primary flavor notes are derived from the leaves of artichokes—it's got a vegetal earthiness hidden under its dark, herbal hood. Artichokes also have the ability to temporarily suspend our perception of sweetness, so when using Cynar in cocktails, it pays to pair it with sweeter items. Benedictine, a sweetened herbal liqueur made by monks, pairs very well with Armagnac, and the blast of peated scotch on top will fill your nose with smoky aromas. It's perfect for sipping on a chilly fall evening, particularly by a fireplace. Herbal, potent, sweet and smokey, this cocktail is truly wtf‽, but in a good way.

1 dash Peychaud's Bitters

.5 oz Cynar

.5 oz Benedictine

.5 oz Armagnac

Spritz of peated Scotch whisky

Stir first 4 ingredients with plenty of ice. Strain into a chilled rocks glass without ice (down). Spray peated Scotch on top.

No garnish.

Sother Says
If you don't have an atomizer, a simple pump spray bottle can stand in just fine.

TAKING A SPRITZ

Unlike the American notion of Happy Hour where we bum rush the bar for two-for-one deals on beers and shots and gorge ourselves on fried snacks, the Italians take a different tack. They have a daily "aperitif hour" where light bodied, low ABV cocktails are coupled with salty finger foods like chips and olives. And no single beverage choice epitomizes this tradition more than the spritz. Popularized in the early 1900s, when soda siphons became readily available, the spritz was originally made by simply combining wine or sparkling wine with seltzer. Eventually, aperitif wines and even amari were added to the lineup for what we now know as a spritz. In Venice, where the habit really began, it was specifically made with the local favorite, Aperitivo Select, but now includes any amaro on offer. Due to some aggressive marketing, Aperol is currently enjoying the top position as the most ordered spritz, but you can also try one featuring Cynar, the amaro that brings the Interrobang‽ together.

Zed is Dead

I've long considered Jamie Boudreau to be my West Coast contemporary. I look back on things I've done in my career, and I see that often at the same time he was doing the exact same thing, a case of coincidence entangled with collective subconscious regarding the trends and techniques that were available. We even share a demeanor that's seen by many as prickly or surly on the outside but (shhhhh) we're actually warm and generous on the inside. Eventually we met and became fast friends.

Jamie owns Canon in Seattle, which tops my list of "Bars I Wish I'd've Opened." They boast the world's largest American whiskey selection and have garnered tons of accolades since opening in 2011. His devotion to the craft expresses itself in interesting, and possibly eccentric ways (example: He took the time [and expense] to stain his bar with Angostura bitters during the Angostura shortage of 2010!), and that attitude carries over to his cocktail creation as well. Zed is Dead, served at Canon in the most aggressive flask you've ever seen, is a prime example. "The cocktail actually started with the glass flask it's served in," says Jamie. "After finding the vessel (inset), I determined something dark, slightly bitter and a with a little bit of a sting at the end was appropriate. As this was created in the fall, we went with Pommeau, a perfect fall/winter ingredient."

Spicy chai-tea infused Cognac pairs beautifully with the bright apple flavors of Pommeau, a blend of apple brandy and fresh apple juice. Bright, bitter citrus is coupled with rich Punt e Mes and just a hint of habanero for a subtle slap to the jowls. "It's extremely complex in flavor, and you don't know what to expect by reading it on paper. And the little kick at the end from the hellfire just puts it over the edge." It's definitely worth waking the gimp for. As for the name, the flask continued to inspire. "The first thing that came to mind when trying to name it was the famous *Pulp Fiction* scene with Butch and Marcellus," says Jamie. "Well, *Fifty Shades* was the first that came to mind, but f*ck that movie." Cheers to that.

1 drop Bittermens Hellfire Habanero Shrub

.25 Galliano apertivo

.5 pommeau

.5 punt e mes

1 oz chai Cognac (pg 247)

Mix and pour into stir•strain•bondage flask*. Refrigerate until ready to serve.

No garnish.

Note: If you can't find this incredibly badass flask, you can also serve this cocktail in a normal one, or neat in a rocks glass.

Milk Punch

2 oz milk

1 oz brown sugar syrup (pg 244)

3 drops vanilla extract

2 oz Armangac

Cocoa nibs and sugar
(coarsely ground nibs mixed
with granulated sugar)

Shake first 4 ingredients with plenty
of ice. Strain into a chilled glass
rimmed with sugar and cocoa nibs.

Garnish with an orange slice.

Sother Says
Most of the Milk Punch recipes
you'll encounter recommend
stirring the drink, but I'm firmly
in the shaken camp on this one.
The milk gets aerated and frothy,
which helps it to be less rich
while creating an irresistible
texture.

My grandfather grew up on a farm and referred to regular milk as "sweet milk" in deference to the buttermilk he'd get fresh from his cows as a boy. When he was younger, he mostly drank scotch whisky neat, but as the old man got on in years he preferred drinks like this one. Enough kick to remind him of his youth but with a distinct, comforting sweetness, I like to ornament the glass with bitter cocoa nibs to balance the sweetness in every sip. It's akin to a boozy milkshake with a lighter body. It's also much less cloying or time-consuming to make than its big brother eggnog. Brandy has a slight cocoa-like quality that to me pairs perfectly with ice cold milk. In the South, where I hail from, it's a common sight at the breakfast table and is always on offer at brunch. I associate milk punch with decadent meals of toasted poppyseed pound cake with homemade chocolate sauce and fluffy biscuits with sawmill gravy. But it's also great on its own, or with like, Cheerios. Whatever you like.

Jack Rose

.5 oz housemade grenadine (pg 245)

.75 oz fresh lime juice

2 oz. Laird's Apple Brandy

Shake and strain into a chilled Cocktail glass.

No garnish.

Sother Says
If you're against making your own grenadine, I recommend buying a bottle from Employees Only.

The Jack Rose is another in the long list of drinks with a dubious history. Was it named by Joseph P. Rose, "World's Champion Mixologist" of the early 1900s or was it invented by (and monikered for) infamous gambler Bald Jack Rose? We may never know. While the jury's still out on its origin story, the verdict is in on whether or not it deserves to be a staple in your repertoire. Fruity, tart and packing a wallop from the 100-proof apple brandy, it's an instant classic, and also one of the first drinks I was compelled to retool. The first thing that should catch your eye is that the Jack Rose only has three ingredients. That's both good and bad news: It implies the drink relies on very little to be great, but when a drink only has three components it's difficult to hide a sub-par ingredient. In this case, the subpar ingredient in question is usually the grenadine, which is why I highly recommend making your own. It's not terribly difficult, and the end result more than makes up for the effort. It's what Bald Jack (or possibly Joseph P. Rose) would have wanted.

The Old Windmill

Amaro Nonino and Montenegro come together to form a juicy layer in this Armagnac-based tipple. The floral and earthy tea bitters combine with the tart rhubarb syrup to give it subtle power, not unlike the slow churning of a long abandoned windmill. Or, if you're feeling less poetic: It's pretty strong. Drink it slow. Fun fact: You can join me for one at my latest project, Windmill, a French-inspired small bar with small bites on New York's Lower East Side

2 dashes 18.21 Earl Grey Bitters

.75 oz rhubarb syrup (pg 244)

.5 oz Amaro Montenegro

.75 oz Amaro Nonino

1 oz Armagnac

Stir all ingredients with plenty of ice to chill and dilute. Strain into a chilled Cocktail glass.

No garnish.

Brandy Alexander

The gin-based original Alexander cocktail, commissioned from New York City barman Troy Alexander of Rector's to launch an ad campaign for cleaner burning coal, has been surpassed by the Brandy Alexander, a decadently creamy and sweet cocktail reminiscent of a boozy milkshake. Brandy's traces of cocoa are propelled forward by the cacao, and the cream gives the drink considerable weight and pleasing depth of flavor. A favorite of the late John Lennon, he was once ejected from L.A.'s Troubadour Club in 1974 for relentlessly heckling the Smothers Brothers. In his apology Lennon said "It was my first night on Brandy Alexanders, and my last." It was not.

.75 oz heavy cream

1 oz Crème de cacao

1.25 oz brandy

Classic COCKTAIL

Shake vigorously with ice to chill dilute and emulsify. Strain into a chilled Cocktail glass.

Garnish with grated nutmeg.

Apricot Julep

As early as 1784, Juleps were thought to be medicinal elixirs, or at least vehicles for delivering medicines for upset stomachs. Though the most revered version is made with bourbon, all manner of spirits as well as wines and fortified wines can be used in a Julep. Breaking it down into its component parts, the Julep has a sweetener, spirit or wine, and an herbal component, which are then served over crushed or pebble ice. The pliable nature of the Julep is advantageous as it allows for variations that are as limitless as the imagination. Which is to say, tinker as you like and find something you love. In this version, apricot preserves and honey syrup serve as the sweetener and mirror some of the flavors present in Armagnac. Thyme is a member of the mint family and is as aromatic though a bit more savory than its cousin. The aromas are mildly woody with hints of citrus, making it complementary to both the sweet-tart apricot and the oaky wood in the Armagnac. Pebble ice melts more quickly than cubes but in a Julep, that's desirable. As you sip, the drink gets softer and more quaffable. I do declare, you'll love it.

.5 oz honey syrup (pg 244)

2 tsp apricot preserves (I use Polaner All Fruit)

2 oz Armagnac

Add all ingredients to a cocktail shaker and add a small amount of pebble ice. Whip shake until the ice melts to aerate and chill. Pour into a Julep cup filled with pebble ice.

Garnish with a sprig of thyme.

Sother Says
Before using fresh herbs to garnish drinks, place them in the palm of your hand and give them a good slap with your other hand, which breaks some of the cell walls and releases volatile oils for a burst of aroma.

Margarita, pg 150

SOURS

The sour is a likely descendant of punch, which stands as a sort of culinary mother sauce in the cocktail lexicon, where just a small addition or subtle change can result in a completely new outcome. Punch, described in rhyme as "one of sour, two of sweet, three of strong and four of weak" could easily be where the sour finds its lineage. Obviously, the proportions are recalibrated to be in individual servings, meaning the ratios are roughly the same just on a smaller scale.

The first written credit for a sour recipe lies in Jerry "Professor" Thomas's 1862 book *The Bartender's Guide*. It contained sugar dissolved with a splash of seltzer water, lemon juice and American whiskey, what we might call a Whiskey Sour today. But it's easy to trace that this style of drink existed well before the publication of his seminal work. In fact, as mentioned in the gin section, a basic earlier version of a sour is likely what kept sailors scurvy-free while out to sea.

In the early 1700s, English naval officer Vice Admiral Edward Vernon commonly wore a long coat made of grogram, a loosely woven woolen fabric of the time. His penchant for doing so earned him the nickname "Old Grog." He's also credited with adding lemon and lime juices to his men's daily rum ration, which helped them avoid contracting scurvy. The juice-diluted rum then took on his nickname of "Grog." Yo-Ho!

But a sour is more than just a cocktail that contains a base spirit or liqueur combined with sweetener and lemon or lime juice; it's a drink that serves as a template for myriad classic and common cocktails. After the aforementioned Whiskey Sour, the likely next in line was the Gin Sour (followed closely by the Gin Fizz, a sour served long with seltzer water). Other well-known cocktails, including the Daiquiri (pg 174), Caipirinha and obviously the Amaretto Sour, a common gateway cocktail, adhere to this simple formula. Few things in life are binary, however, and the sour is no exception. If we can agree that the template is spirit, sweetener and citrus, then we can make more complex sours while still coloring within the lines.

The Ward 8 is a great example. A whiskey-based sour, it features grenadine as its sweetener and both orange and lemon juice as the sour aspects. The White Lady (a favorite of mine) and the Sidecar both use triple sec as their sweet component, making for a drier and boozier gin or brandy sour, respectively. Even the venerable Margarita (pg 151), the sour that made it big, uses Cointreau over simple syrup. Note: This doesn't stop bartenders all over the country from adding high fructose corn syrup to their Margs in the form of pre-made Margarita mix (though my opinion is that it should).

Another example of playing with the format comes from Peru with the Pisco Sour, featuring—you guessed it—pisco, a geographically significant spirit made from grapes. But pisco isn't the only thing unique about this cocktail. Though not specifically called for in the original recipe, the addition of egg white is considered canon in most craft cocktail bars, transforming this scrappy, rakish tipple into a tamer, more refined sipper. The addition of egg whites create a light, fluffy mouthfeel, and the bitters dashed on top add a delightful aroma.

We shouldn't talk about sours without at least mentioning the Daisy. The first recipe utilizing the name was printed in the 1876 second edition of Thomas's aforementioned book. The Brandy Daisy calls for gomme syrup, Curaçao, lemon, brandy and a dash of Jamaican rum shaken together and strained into an ice-filled Collins glass topped with seltzer. A subset of the sour, Daisies are served long with seltzer like a Fizz, but contain both a sweetener and a liqueur modifier and almost always rely on lemon juice as the sour component. In effect, they're a fancy sour. And damned delicious.

I've also been known to age sours from time to time. I built one using brandy, orange, lemon and lime juices and demerara sugar. I stowed them all in large glass bottles and have been cracking a few open on New Year's Eve ever since (I'm currently awaiting year five!).

The key to playing around with this format is to maintain the ratio I mentioned earlier and to work with flavors that work for you. A standard sour is practically bulletproof. Any way you choose to serve them, they rarely disappoint.

Parisian Sour

This riff on the Pisco Sour is built around two beloved French exports, Cognac and vermouth, which—like pisco—both start their lives as grapes. Combining them in a cocktail seems elementary to me. Plus, so many Cognacs have cocoa mentioned in their flavor profile that it makes it equally obvious to me to add chocolate bitters to the mix, though I reserve them for garnishing the top of the drink as it's their aroma that'll do the work of pushing the flavor of the Cognac into the spotlight. And, don't worry, the strength of the 106 proof Royer dispels any notion that this drink is too sweet. The fluffy texture provided by the egg white balances the mouthfeel for a delightful sour.

Egg white	2 oz Louis Royer Force 53 Cognac
.5 oz cane syrup	
.5 oz lemon juice	Chocolate bitters
.75 oz Dolin Blanc Vermouth	

Dry shake the egg white, then shake the next 4 ingredients over ice. Strain into a chilled Coup glass.

Garnish with chocolate bitters.

THE Philly Sling

Derek Brown operates the Columbia Room in our nation's capital, a bar I've taken several cues from in the establishment of my own programs, and also helms the wildly successful PUB or Pop-Up Bar, an establishment that changes identity and theme several times each year. Additionally, he's "the highest ranking bartender in U.S. Government," as he's the Chief Spirits Advisor for the National Archives. He makes an exceptional martini, and he's a fantastic conversationalist over bottles of beer and shots of whiskey.

He sent me his cocktail the Philly Sling, so named because he thought it'd sound like a classic cocktail (and also because his friend and fellow bartender Phoebe Esmon lived in Philly at the time), and I've been obsessing over it ever since. "I wanted a simple drink at the Columbia Room that incorporated Sloe Gin but that wasn't already on the books," says Derek. Sloe Gin is made by soaking blackthorn drupes (they look like small plums) in gin, and the resulting flavor is that of sweet dark fruit and juniper.

"I love the way Sloe Gin tastes like a crisp apple when you add Calvados (France's reknowned apple brandy) and lemon juice," says Derek. "It's a sour for people who don't want a long drink or even, really, much of a sour element. From there, I added bitters to give it more of a kick. It was fun working through the best proportions—this one can go off the rails quickly! Sometimes bartenders get hung up on making drinks that slice your cheeks off from the acid. I don't like to go there. This was the perfect balance for my taste."

If you're interested in trying this one at home (and you should be, because it's fantastic), I recommend Plymouth Sloe Gin, as it's the best and most traditional on the market. Though some American brands are producing good products using similar drupes, many makers simply use flavoring agents and neutral spirits to make what I feel are inferior versions. I'm certain Derek would agree—and you should trust him: He's been bowling at the White House!

---

1 dash Fee Brothers Whiskey Barrel-Aged Bitters

.25 oz simple syrup

.5 oz fresh lemon juice

1 oz Plymouth Sloe Gin

1.5 oz Calvados

Shake all ingredients with ice. Strain into a chilled Cocktail glass.

Garnish with an apple chip.

Take Me to Marrakech

Still produced in incredibly limited amounts, Armangac is somewhat difficult to find in the U.S. However, it's not impossible, and I encourage you to be adventurous and seek it out. If your liquor store doesn't carry any, start a relationship with the owner and ask him to stock it for you. For this drink, I recommend a younger Armagnac like Baron Francois VS, Comte de Lauvia or Baron de Sigognac VS as they will have flavors of quince, apricot and even prune that mingle well with the juices and honey syrup. All of these notes will balance out the savory and citrusy complexity of the Cardamom bitters. Each of these flavor notes is reminiscent of the heady aromas and flavors of Morocco and, what at first glance seems a simple combination suddenly becomes more than the sum of its parts, requiring no further adornment.

2 dashes Scrappy's Cardamom Bitters

.5 oz orange juice

.5 oz lemon juice

.5 oz honey syrup

1.5 oz Armagnac

Shake and strain into a chilled Cocktail glass.

No garnish.

GraviTea

The name of this drink was borne out of one of those stream of consciousness word associations those of us who regularly create cocktails are forced to engage in ("Tastes like tea and Fig Newtons…Newton's Law… Gravity…'GraviTea.' That'll work.") Trust me, naming them is much harder than creating, or in this case, drinking them. Armagnac is the backbone of this fall stunner, which gains an herbal accent from the Bénédictine with sweet and savory notes from the figs. The bitters-infused cream is icing on the cake. Whatever you choose to call it, enjoy!

2 tsp fig jam (I use Bonne Maman)	1 oz heavy cream
.5 oz Bénédictine	2 dashes AZ Bitters Lab Figgy Pudding Bitters
1.5 oz Armagnac	
3 oz Rooibos tea	

Put the first 3 ingredients into a cocktail shaker with ice and shake vigorously to break up the jam, chill and dilute. Strain into a Collins glass filled 3/4 with ice. Top with tea and gently stir to incorporate.

Pour cream and bitters into a clean shaker and shake vigorously for 15 seconds to whip. Layer the cream atop the drink.

No garnish.

Saint Jacques District

Fruity and floral grenadine is heightened by Cointreau and orange bitters in this tribute to our French neighbors to the north. Cognac and lemon juice give tartness and strength to balance out the concoction. This is a drink for the long days of late summer, which those who live in Canada get to enjoy a little longer than the rest of us.

2 dashes Regan's Orange Bitters No. 6	.5 oz grenadine
.5 oz lemon juice	.5 oz Cointreau
	2 oz Cognac

Pour all ingredients into a cocktail shaker and add plenty of ice. Shake vigorously to chill and dilute. Strain into a chilled Cocktail glass.

Garnish with an orange twist.

Café Brûlée

Vanilla, burnt sugar and smoked salt come together to give this Cognac Old Fashioned a greater depth. Brooding yet playful, it's a perfect complement to an after-dinner pipe or cigar, or whatever you choose to enjoy for dessert. Just know that the coffee will likely serve to offer a jolt, enlivening your late evening (or early morning) conversation.

.5 oz cold brew coffee	2 dashes vanilla bitters
1.5 tsp burnt sugar syrup (pg 245)	Pinch smoked salt or Maldon salt
1.5 oz Cognac	

In a double Old Fashioned glass add first 4 ingredients. Place a large lump of ice in the glass and gently stir to combine. Sprinkle the salt on top.

No garnish.

DRINKING TEQUILA IS MORE ABOUT THE JOURNEY THAN THE DESTINATION

— RAINBOW ROWELL

Tequila

təˈkēlə / noun

1. a kind of mezcal, produced in specific states of Mexico and made from mashed and fermented blue agave

2. the Devil's water

3. a song by The Champs you know all the words to

ON TEQUILA & MEZCAL

Agave-based booze goes way beyond the Margarita.

Tequila is maligned more often than any other spirit. Even some of the most stalwart imbibers I know have a "one time I had too much tequila" story that has turned them off the stuff for good. The golden-hued, mass-produced, inexpensive tequila that was (well, is) a free-flowing staple at college parties across the land is one explanation for stomach-churning reactions to the stuff. The ritual of taking a shot of tequila—the salt, the shot, the lime squeeze—that's been perpetuated in pop culture also makes a shot of tequila more fun to order than say, a shot of whisk(e)y, and the more shots of something you consume the better the chances you're going to have a horror story about it. And yet, the most iconic of all tequila drinks, the Margarita, remains the most ordered mixed drink in the country, which speaks either to the tempting resilience of the spirit even among people who've had a bad experience with it or an absolute devotion to it among those of us who don't turn green every time we get a whiff. The truth is it's probably a little bit of both.

To continue our "all spirits start as vodka" premise, tequila and mezcal (I'll define the differences in a bit) are "vodka" made specifically from the agave plant. Sometimes the agave is steamed prior to fermentation, other times it's roasted. After distillation, it is often (but not always) aged in oak barrels. Tequila's origins can be traced back to the 16th century. Before the arrival of the conquistadors, Mexico hadn't distilled any spirits. In fact, it's worth noting tequila was the first distilled spirit in all of North America. As the Spanish soldiers exhausted their supplies of brandy, they targeted the agave plant as a potentially distillable product. Lucky for us, they nailed it.

Tequila can only be produced in Jalisco and a few municipalities in the states of Guanajuato, Michoacán, Nayarit and Tamaulipas. It's also recognized as a Mexican Designation of Origin by more than 40 countries, thus protecting it from being imitated elsewhere in the world. Tequila can only be made from the blue agave plant native to the region. There are two categories within this rule, 100% agave, and mixtos, which must be at least 51% agave—the rest of the distillate can be comprised of other sugars. While I'm not in the business of telling you how to live your life, I do recommend avoiding mixtos overall and sticking with 100% agave tequila. They taste better, they have no additives and you'll generally get a better quality beverage for your buck whether drinking them straight or mixing that classic Marg. I should also note Jose Cuervo, one of the aforementioned, yellow-hued ghosts of frat parties past—is a mixto. If Cuervo is your favorite tequila, I suggest branching out a bit into the 100% agave offerings. Your palate and your liver will thank you.

So how does the agave plant, a succulent similar to overgrown aloe that grows in dry red clay soil, become a bottle of booze? The process begins with

A group of jimadors loading up harvested blue agave in the town of Tequila, Jalisco, Mexico.

gathering the piña, the heart of the agave plant. Based on its size and growth patterns, the piña is practically impossible to cultivate or harvest mechanically. As a result, the process of farming agave is laborious and has remained largely unchanged by time. The farmers who steward the plant to maturity and then harvest it by hand are called a jimadors. Agave plants aren't ready for harvest until they are between 6 and 12 years old and are between 150 and 250 pounds. The piña, so called because it resembles a pineapple, grows at the center of the plant and is covered with long flat leaves with sharp points on the end similar to an aloe plant crossed with the Spanish bayonet plant. They look angry. In order to get to the piña those leaves must be removed by hand using a coa, a round blade on the end of a long handle. Because the plants mature at different rates of speed, it's up to the jimador to determine which ones to harvest and which ones to allow to continue to grow, a skill best learned through experience.

On a visit to Mexico a few years ago, at the Avión distillery, I was given the opportunity to attempt the process. After only one agave I was sweating and short of breath, and all I'd done was cut off the leaves—if I were a jimador I'd have also been responsible for loading each piña I'd processed into a truck to get it to the distillery. Somehow the jimadors routinely process more than 100 agave per day while simultaneously trimming and caring for other plants along the way. The grueling nature of the work as well as the fact that the skills required to be an effective jimador are passed down from generation to generation is actually leading to a crisis in the region. The children of jimadors are increasingly less interested in taking on the family business because, frankly, it's backbreaking work that doesn't pay particularly well. As a result, many tequila and mezcal distilleries are reinvesting in these laborers, incentivizing the position in an effort to create a sustainability of personnel as well as to preserve the heritage of the craft.

This interest in sustainability manifests itself in other ways as well. Mexican distillers are leading the industry in methods to lessen their impact on the environment. For example, pulp and fibers left over after extracting the juice from the agave plants are used as animal feed, burned as fuel (sometimes to fire the stills) and even made into paper and rope.

Once it's been harvested, the piña is cut in half or quarters to aid in even cooking, and stacked into large ovens and steam baked slowly to break down its natural sugars. After steaming for 24 to 48 hours, the piña is allowed to cool for an additional 24 hours or more. Then they're crushed to press out the juice. Traditionally this aspect of the process takes place in a tahona, a large mortar with a giant stone grinding wheel that's pulled around by a donkey. This method is preferred over mechanical extraction as it doesn't over extract the juice, which helps keep the unwanted flavors from the flesh out of the end product. Some distilleries have mechanized the stone wheel while others sacrifice quality for speed by using a shredding machine to extract the juices, which often leads to some of those unwanted flavors slipping through.

Where the agave was grown also has an impact on the flavor of the tequila. Highland agaves yield a sweeter, fruiter flavor while agave from the lowlands are vegetal and earthy.

Once extracted, the juice is collected into vats and fermented for several days. The resulting wort, or *mosto* in Spanish, must be distilled twice by law. Some makers distill a third time to create a final product that is cleaner in flavor, possibly to market to the American palate. However, after the second distillation, it's ready to bottle as Blanco tequila or to be aged in order to create a different style.

There are four classifications referring to the age of the tequila, and each have characteristic flavors and aromas associated with them, outlined below.

When discussing the aging of tequila, it's important to think about the ambient temperature and how it compares to the temperature of other aging regions of the distilling world. If we think of the planet as an oven, it's got a hot spot, a cold spot and a sweet spot just like your oven at home. So, the spirit will "age" approximately the same when barrelled for three years in the hot spot of Mexico where tequila hails from as it would in seven years

The Four Classifications of Tequila...

Blanco (White)
Typically bottled right off the still, by law it can sit for up to two months in stainless steel or wooden casks. Many distillers choose to use this two-month period to marry flavors from multiple distillations to ensure consistency. It's also often called "plata" or "silver" tequila, and has a bright, crisp flavor, with herbal notes of cilantro and hints of spice like black pepper. This is the perfect style tequila for Margaritas and palomas as it's got plenty of fresh aromas and flavors that mingle well with the other ingredients in those cocktails.

Reposado (Rested)
These tequilas must be aged at least two months but for no more than one year in oak barrels of any size up to 20,000 liters. The result is a slightly mellowed tequila with hints of oak and vanilla suited for Old Fashioneds

or other stirred, spirit-forward applications like a Tequila Manhattan.

Añejo (Aged)
Rested for a minimum of one year but less than three in small oak barrels (usually standard-sized casks of 200 liters) distillers typically rest añejo tequila in barrels previously used by American whiskey producers. As a result, Anejo tequila has hints of caramel, cooked agave and back-notes of spice and pepper. Enjoy these beauties neat or with a little ice.

Extra Añejo (Extra Aged)
A relatively new classification implemented in 2006, these tequilas are aged for more than three years. I recommend sipping these neat in a snifter, as you might a rare scotch or fine Cognac, to capture their aroma.

in the sweet spot of the southeast United States where bourbon and rye are aged, compared to 14 years in the cool spot of Scotland's scotch regions.

Speaking of scotch, which brings to mind subtle hints of smoky—let's start back at the beginning of the tequila-making process to discuss tequila's typically smokier cousin, mezcal. Though I discussed tequila first, as it's more familiar to most people, tequila is a subset of mezcal. While tequila must be made using the blue agave, mezcal is the name given to any agave-based spirit—and there are more than 30 varieties commonly used in mezcal production. The process dates back more than 200 years and its methodology has been handed down from generation to generation. Making mezcal is largely the same as making tequila, with one major difference. Instead of steaming the piña, mezcal distillers—also known as mezcaleros—roast them in earthen pits. The pits are roughly 10 feet wide and 10 feet deep and lined with stones. The mezcaleros build a wood fire in the pit to heat the stones, at which point they add the quartered or halved piñas. They cover the roasting piñas with a layer of damp burlap and then cover the whole pit with earth. The smoke from the embers combined with the heat of the stones, cooks and flavors the piña, giving mezcal a signature smokiness.

After two to three days, the piña is pulled from the pit and crushed in the tahona just like those for tequila. The juice is then fermented and twice distilled. Copper pot stills are often employed, but a more traditional method is the clay pot still, which imparts an even earthier tone to the mezcal. Typically, mezcal that is bottled without aging is called joven. A few mezcals are aged up to four years and rarely, up to 12. The scarcity of long-aged mezcal is mainly driven by economics, as the need for capital outweighs the desire to wait for the product to age this long. As such, these entries can be pretty pricey.

Similar to tequila, there is the 100% agave variety and mixto, but for mezcal, mixtos must be

Stones are thrown into a pit of roasting piñas in the San Baltazar Guelavila region of Oaxaca, Mexico.

comprised of 80% agave instead of the 51% for tequila. Within both categories there are four age statements. Joven or white, isn't aged at all. Dorado or golden (almost always a mixto) has a coloring agent added. Reposado/añejado is barrel-aged for a minimum of two months and up to nine. It doesn't take on a great deal of flavor from the barrel in those shorter times but is still slightly mellowed. Añejo is aged for a minimum of 12 months but, if it's 100% agave, it's typically aged for four years.

Mezcal is made in nine specific regions of Mexico to meet its Appellation of Origin: Oaxaca, Durango, Guanajuato, Guerrero, San Luis Potosi, Tamaulipas, Zacatecas, Michoacan and Puebla, three of which overlap with tequila's regions. Oaxaca is by far the largest producer, responsible for around 85% of all mezcal.

One of the most challenging things about mezcal is exploring the variety within the category. Flavors can vary depending on the variety of agave used, any herbs or fruits that may be added during fermentation and the chosen distilling method. Though most mezcal is simply distilled and bottled, there are subcategories including pechuga or "breast," where the distillate is passed through a chicken, duck or turkey breast and seasoned with winter spices and fruits. Other (numerous) varieties are named after the specific agave used.

Mezcal can be consumed in any way you feel speaks to you. It's been cropping up in drinks in the U.S. for years, particularly in cocktails such as the Oaxaca Old Fashioned. Due to its powerful and distinct flavor, I recommend using a judicious hand if you're mixing it with other spirits—a little goes a long way. Outside the states, mezcal is typically taken neat with a slice of citrus fruit (I prefer grapefruit) dusted with chili and sal de gusano.

What's sal de gusano? The English translation, worm salt, should add a bit of clarity. The worm in this case is actually the larvae of moths that feed on the agave plant, and as they get fattened up on a steady diet of agave nectar, they make an excellent source of protein. Sal de gusano is made by toasting these larvae then grinding them up with rock salt and dried chile peppers. It's delicious, and an authentic way to enjoy mezcal. It's also part of the reason some people associate worms with a bottle of agave-based spirit. The worm, usually either a gusano rojo ("red worm") or a chinicuil ("maguey worm," the caterpillar of the Hypopta agavis moth), allegedly was added in an effort to differentiate mezcal from tequila. Some claimed adding the worm lent more complex flavors to the mezcal, while others made the case eating the worm at the bottom of your bottle was good luck or an aphrodisiac, which is to say, good luck. Either way, both interpretations are best considered marketing gimmicks. Don't fall for it—the good stuff sells itself. If your mezcal has a worm in it, there's a pretty good chance it's cheap hooch. If your tequila has a worm in it, there's an even better chance it's a bad bottle: The Normas Oficiales Mexicanas (the Mexican Standards authority) prohibits the addition of worms or larvae to tequila, meaning if you find one in yours, someone slipped it in long after it was bottled. Best to leave it alone.

But don't skip tequila or mezcal forever just because you had a bad bout with a worse bottle. And if you can't stand it straight, I have some ideas....

Retox with the Margarita

A popular fad known as the Detox Cleanse requires its devotees to drink a mixture of lemon juice, maple syrup and cayenne pepper for several days to offer health benefits and aid in weight loss. Though its proponents swear by the practice, I'd prefer to see an actual doctor and visit the gym rather than subject myself to such lengths. But the detox mixture was so close in nature to a simple sour that I felt compelled to use it as the inspiration for a riff on the classic Margarita. Fresh jalapeños stand in for the cayenne pepper for a brighter, more vegetal flavor, and the richness of maple syrup combined with the tart lemon juice creates palette confusion and beckons you back for more. It might not be as healthy, but life's too short to skip a drink this good.

RETOX

2–3 slices of fresh jalapeño

.75 oz grade B maple syrup

.5 oz fresh lemon juice

2 oz reposado tequila

Kosher salt for rim

Muddle jalapeño in base of tin, add syrup, lemon and tequila. Shake vigorously with ice. Double strain (to remove any pepper bits) into a half salted rim glass of fresh ice.

Garnish with lemon slice.

MARGARITA

1 oz lime juice

.75 oz Cointreau

2 oz blanco tequila
(I prefer Altos)

Rim half a double rocks glass with kosher salt. Combine ingredients into a shaker with ice and shake to chill and dilute. Strain and serve over ice in salt-rimmed glass.

Garnish with lime wedge.

MARGARITAS

Tequila is a polarizing spirit. So many people have stories about why they "can't drink tequila anymore." I blame youthful overindulgence as well as poor quality for this affliction. Still, according to Drinks International, as of 2017, the Margarita ranks as the seventh most ordered alcoholic beverage in the world. Which is to say, not everyone has issues with tequila (or at least those who don't are more than willing to pick up the slack for those who do). Like most classics, a well made Margarita is a stellar concoction with very few ingredients: tequila, fresh lime juice and a sweetener like triple sec. Though the scant ingredient list makes it tough to hide a bad one, it's a very forgiving mixture and the ratios can vary widely depending on your desired outcome. Like it more tart? Increase the lime and decrease the triple sec. For sweeter? Do the opposite. Just don't forget the salt. ¡Olé!

Frozen Smoke

Thanks to a renewed interest in tiki culture as a subset of the mixology revolution, the blender has made a triumphant return to the back bar. However, frozen drinks are a bit of an oxymoron as spiritus alcohol has such a low freezing point. To compensate for the dilution that takes place as a result of blending so much ice with booze, frozen/blender drinks are typically larger in volume—which explains why your typical frozen Marg is twice the size of the one you might have ordered on the rocks. The Frozen Smoke is essentially a Margarita upgrade for the personal humidor set. There are two layers of smoke in this cocktail. The first comes from the inherent smokiness of mezcal and the second comes via the technique of cold smoking the pineapple juice. This creates a dynamic juxtaposition of frosty and toasty to confuse and delight the palate. Though there is a considerable amount of extra work involved in this cocktail, the results will be outstanding for you and your guests. After all, no one breaks out the blender to make just one drink!

.75 oz smoked pineapple juice

.75 oz lime juice

.5 oz passion fruit syrup (pg 244)

.25 oz Ancho Reyes

.5 oz Vida mezcal

1.5 oz Olmeca Altos Blanco tequila

Blend with ice until smooth. Pour into a glass and serve.

Garnish with grilled pineapple and edible flowers.

SMOKING STUFF

Smoked cocktails are continuing to gain popularity and for good reason: They're delicious. I personally prefer to smoke components of a cocktail, like juice, rather than the whole thing. It's relatively simple to do. Pour whatever liquid you want to smoke into a shallow pan and seal with plastic wrap. Poke a small hole at both ends. Using a Smoking Gun, pipe smoke into one of the holes until it's billowing out of the other. Remove the tube and cover both holes. Allow to sit until the smoke is no longer visible inside the plastic wrap, then pour or store as you see fit. The Smoking Gun is a handy tool to have around the kitchen or bar (and only costs about $80).

Mezcal Swizzle

Though not technically a swizzle, as I employ a mixing method known as the "whip and dirty" shake to mix it, this is still a long aerated drink served over packed pebble ice. It's smokey from the mezcal, slightly nutty and off-dry from the sherry and closes out with fresh fruit flavors and a spicy burst from the fresh ginger. All those flavors are balanced through the warm island spices in the falernum. The whole package is a complex taste of the tropics in an approachable, easy drinking package. I encourage you to set aside your preconceptions and try the sal de gusano (aka "Worm Salt") garnish if you can acquire it, as it adds another layer of nuttiness and complexity. It's also the authentic way to enjoy mezcal.

.5 oz lime juice

.5 oz grapefruit juice

.5 oz homemade falernum (pg 244)

.5 oz ginger syrup (pg 244)

1 oz Amontillado sherry

1 oz mezcal

Combine all ingredients with a few pieces of pebble ice. Whip and dirty shake until ice is melted, then pour into a Collins glass and add pebble ice.

Garnish with grapefruit and sal de gusano.

SHERRY, BABY

A generally misunderstood fortified wine from Jerez, Spain, sherry has an incredible range, from bone dry through to syrupy sweet. After fermentation, grape spirits are added (fortification) and then some are allowed to age in a system called solera. Picture a pyramid of barrels with the new-make wine in the top barrel. The row below has some new-make wine as well as some of the previous year's wine in it. The third row has some wine from the second row as well as some from the year(s) prior, and wine is bottled from the bottom row without ever fully emptying the barrel. The aging allows oxidation to take place and adds a richness to the final product, while the system of fractional blending increases the average age of sherry over time and ensures consistency as it basically homogenizes the liquid year after year. Sherries are excellent drinking wines and, because of their range, can be very handy in designing cocktails as well.

Ricardo Zarza

Storied London bartender Dick Bradsell created several neo-classic cocktails, and chief among them is the Bramble. A charismatic and engaging man, he is said to have single-handedly changed the face of the London cocktail scene in the '80s. This drink pays homage to him but substitutes tequila for the standard gin, hence its name*. The result is an earthier, less herbal cocktail than the original, while still maintaining the subtle sweetness from blackberries and a tart jolt provided by fresh citrus juice. The crème de mûre is the lynchpin of the drink, transforming it into a nostalgia-driven sno-cone for adults.

.75 oz fresh lime juice

.5 oz simple syrup

1.5 oz Olmeca Altos Blanco tequila

.75 oz crème de mûre

Fill a Rocks glass with crushed ice and add the first 3 ingredients; stir to combine. Add more crushed ice if needed and carefully drizzle the crème de mûre on top.

Garnish with blackberries.

Sother Says
Sub the tequila out for gin and swap the lime juice in favor of lemon: That's the original Bramble.

*For those who don't habla español, Ricardo Zarza is Spanish for "Richard (occasionally shortened to Dick) Bramble."

Chain Smoker

This is basically a smoky mezcal Manhattan augmented with Zucca, an Italian aperitif, which has a natural smoky flavor from the dried Chinese rhubarb that serves as its base ingredient. The bitters add a subtle citrus note as well as another layer of smoke. Finally, the garnish adds a burnt oil slick on top of the drink itself. A chain of smoky flavors. Ask me again how we come up with names for cocktails.

2 dashes Cocktailpunk Smoked Orange Bitters

.25 oz Zucca Rabarbaro

.75 oz dry vermouth

2 oz mezcal

Stir all ingredients with plenty of ice to chill and dilute. Strain into a chilled Rocks glass without ice.

Garnish with a flamed orange twist.

Hemingway's Cats

This is a simple sour recipe that reimagines a formiddable classic. A mezcal spin on the Hemingway Daiquiri (pg 174), this version has a distinct smoky flavor. Maraschino, made from cherry pits, has a marzipan-like flavor and the black lemon bitters, actually made from dried limes, are dusky and drying. This cocktail may not be for everyone, but then again neither are cats—and they're doing just fine.

2 dashes Scrappy's Black Lemon Bitters

.25 oz grapefruit juice

.5 oz agave syrup

.5 oz lime juice

.5 oz Maraschino liqueur

2 oz mezcal

Shake all ingredients with plenty of ice to chill and dilute. Strain into a chilled Cocktail glass.

Garnish with a thin lime wheel.

Bee's Thing

Pulling inspiration from both the Bee's Knees, a classic gin cocktail (pg. 51) and the Bee Sting, a spicy riff on the classic powered by Ancho Reyes chile liqueur, this zippy agave lemonade is bolstered by rich reposado tequila and accented with herbal Génépy. It'll have you buzzing in no time.

2 thin slices of fresh jalapeño

.25 oz dark agave syrup

.75 oz lemon juice

1.5 tsp of Génépy

1.5 oz reposado tequila

Muddle the jalapeño in the base of a cocktail shaker. Add remaining ingredients and plenty of ice. Shake vigorously to further break up the pepper. Double strain into a chilled Cocktail glass to remove all bits of pepper.

No garnish.

THOUGHTS ON ICE

The most underappreciated ingredient in your cocktail is frozen water.

'**S**other," my regulars occasionally ask, "why do your drinks taste better than the ones I make at home?"

"Because I do the dishes," is my simple reply. And while it's true there's a joy inherent in not having to clean the glassware and wipe the bottles down after a few drinks, there's another reason a cocktail made to the exact same specs will taste better at my bar than at my apartment: The bar's got better ice.

We use a Kold-Draft machine, as do most establishments that are serious about the quality of their cocktails. That's because, with very few exceptions, ice is a major component of every cocktail you'll ever make or drink. Whether being stirred or shaken with it to prepare the drink or built and served over it or in some cases blended with the stuff, ice is an often overlooked yet powerful presence in the world of mixed drinks. Kold-Draft comes closest to replicating ice you'd find in the wild.

As recently as 1790, ice was considered a luxury only for the wealthy and elite (and those who lived in climates where it occurred naturally and often), due to the fact that harvesting it by hand from frozen lakes was an incredibly labor-intensive process. Men used hand saws and pickaxes to chisel it out. It then had to be insulated and packed tightly with sawdust so it wouldn't melt on its journey, but as you can probably imagine a great deal of it did anyway. The ice that was still ice would then be stored in a cool, dry space until it was needed.

I'm sure the tables and bars it finally made its debut upon were lovely affairs, but it's an awful lot of trouble and expense just to be able to enjoy a cold drink. Still, people happily paid the price, and believe it or not, the ice they received was of better quality than that produced in our modern-day freezers.

Unlike what happens in our freezer, ice formed in a lake undergoes what's known as "directional freezing," meaning that as the ambient temperature begins to drop, ice forms on the surface of the water and begins to freeze downward toward the lakebed beneath. This process happens pretty slowly, gently forcing oxygen, particulate matter and other impurities trapped in solution toward the bottom of the lake and out of the ice. The result is solid water that's incredibly dense and clear as glass.

Because modern freezers and conventional ice makers create ice so quickly, oxygen doesn't have time to escape—which explains those big white clouds present in nearly every cube. And if the air inside your freezer is trapped inside your ice, that means the smell inside your freezer is trapped inside it too. The scents of the year-old frozen turkey leg you've been meaning to thaw out, the wet cardboard tang of a nearly finished Häagen-Dazs pint and that weird blue gel pack you use when you tweak your knee all intertwine in the ice and infiltrate your cocktail as it begins to melt. And because the ice has air pockets inside it, it'll melt faster than ice created in the natural world.

If you're particular about ice—and you should be, given everything you just learned—you may want to consider freezing it in a sealable container on its own, away from the other contaminants in your freezer. If possible, store your ice in the freezer until ready to use. This will keep it from tempering, which is a fancy way to say "no longer in a state of freezing." Tempered ice accumulates a layer of moisture on all its surfaces, which can dilute your beverage faster than you'd like before chilling it as much as is necessary. Plus, when softened, ice melts at a greater rate of speed.

For stirring and shaking drinks, I prefer cubes that are approximately one inch on all sides. Fill your shaker 2/3 full and shake vigorously for approximately 20 seconds for any drinks served up, and 15 seconds for drinks served on the rocks. For stirred, fill the mixing glass until you have enough ice to keep the bottom layer of ice submerged and stir briskly for 15 seconds for drinks served up. If your ice is particularly dense, consider cracking the first piece that goes into the mixing glass to increase surface area and aid in dilution. For drinks served over ice, reduce your stirring time appropriately knowing the drink will continue to dilute once you serve it.

As far as the ice shape that's appropriate for the drink you're making, consider both the makeup and method of the drink. Single large format cubes, spheres and spears are perfect for straight pours of spirit or Old Fashioned style cocktails as they'll melt (read: dilute) slowly. A shaken drink like a Margarita benefits from smaller cubes so that the aeration of the cocktail has nooks and crannies to adhere to, creating a more inviting texture. This is also true of highballs mixed with seltzer or sodas. However, a long clear bar of ice cut to shape for a Collins glass makes for an impressive Japanese highball. These are just suggested guidelines. In the end, do what best suits your aesthetic or whatever you can get your hands on.

And clean out your freezer. It's probably a mess.

Cerveza DEL Reyes
aka "The Kings' Beer"

.25 oz housemade hot sauce (pg 247)

.5 oz Vida mezcal

1 oz Olmeca Altos Reposado

Spicy-sweet salt (p. 247)

Tecate or similar beer

Pour first 3 ingredients into a Highball glass that's rimmed with lime juice and spicy-sweet salt. Add ice and top up with beer. Serve remaining beer on the side with a small bottle of the hot sauce and lime wedge for the guest to use.

Garnish with a lime wedge.

I love this drink on a sunny afternoon. It's a turbo charged michelada* that employs the smokiness of mezcal as well as the punch of tequila with a light-bodied, crisp beer. Dressed with lime juice and homemade hot sauce and served long over ice, I especially like adding more beer and hot sauce as I drink it, giving the cocktail the added appeal of flavor evolution (unless, you know, you chug it). The spicy-sweet salt keeps you coming back for sip after sip until it's time to make another.

BEER: A COCKTAIL'S BEST FRIEND

Beer has so many flavor profiles that its potential as an addition to a drink is virtually unending. It's an easy substitute for seltzer or a soda but, you can further extrapolate the notion to include cocktails that involve sparkling wines as well. I'm fond of the European habit of adding amaro to a light bodied beer and began experimenting with more complex combinations from there. Try making a Seelbach (pg 98) with a nut brown ale! Don't feel like you can't alter a beer a bit either. Reduce a hoppy IPA down to make a floral and bitter syrup for use in tiki drinks, or do the same to an oatmeal stout for ice cream.

*Michela is a slang term for "my beer" in Spanish and helada means frosty or icy. Thus the the word michelada roughly translates to "my iced beer."

Teatro with the Bijou

Teatro, Spanish for theater, is a spin on the classic Bijou cocktail. Bijou, in addition to once being a popular name for theaters and movie houses in the U.S., is also the French word for jewel, and its name is meant to represent the cocktail's main ingredients: gin represents diamonds, Chartreuse represents emeralds and sweet vermouth represents rubies. Stirred together in equal parts and served up, it's quite a delicious concoction. When I was building a menu and looking to fill a slot with a tequila drink, I decided to play around with the Bijou recipe because I love the combination of tequila and herbal liqueurs. The sweet vermouth adds a richness and the bitters bring in a slight citrus note that binds everything together. Though it's an all spirit drink, the Teatro may feel too flabby on your palate, so feel free to shake this one so it's aerated and lighter in texture.

TEATRO

2 dashes orange bitters

1 oz sweet vermouth

1 oz green Chartreuse

1 oz Olmeca Altos Tequila Blanco

Stir all ingredients with ice. Strain into a Cocktail glass over ice.

Garnish with cherries.

BIJOU

1 dash orange bitters

.75 oz sweet vermouth

.75 oz green Chartreuse

.75 oz London Dry gin

Pour all ingredients into a mixing glass and top with plenty of ice. Stir to chill and dilute. Strain into a chilled Cocktail glass.

Garnish with a cherry.

THE 7th Planet
aka the Puck Uranus

One could say Rick Dobbs made the jump from being an IT professional to becoming a bar owner out of necessity—he may have lost his sanity otherwise. He's told me numerous times the notion came to him as he was in a 2 p.m. meeting regarding his 3 p.m. phone call about his 4 p.m. meeting, and he had to get out of that cycle. Currently, Rick, along with his wife, Theresa, owns and operates two incredible neighborhood bars in Livermore, California, the Last Word and the Aviation Rooftop Bar & Kitchen. The ethos at both establishments is built around genuine hospitality with menus focused on classic cocktails. Rick is known as a quick-witted joker with a larger-than-life personality, and his aim is to put his guests into a better mindset than the one they came in with, whether through good humor or good drinks. This cocktail and its origin story are a small example of how Rick is capable of producing both simultaneously. "My wife and I did this event at the Academy of Sciences at which all of the drinks had to be centered around something science-related and we had to decorate our table," says Rick. "I wanted to make the whole thing like a third grade science fair project around Uranus. I also wanted to point out that all of the moons of Uranus were named after characters from Shakespeare's plays. Thus, the 'Puck Uranus' was born. But the sponsor for the event was having none of it. Thus 'Puck Uranus' died and '7th Planet' was born." Essentially a smokey blue margarita topped with a luxurious Prosecco float, in my opinion this one's pucking good enough to carry two names.

1 oz lime juice

.5 oz Giffard Blue Curaçao

2 oz Olmeca Altos Reposado

Prosecco

Combine all ingredients except Prosecco into a shaker with ice and shake well. Strain into an ice-filled Highball glass. Top with Prosecco.

Garnish with a lime wheel.

Mango Cilantro Habanero or "MCH"

If you haven't realized by now, I'll just come out and say it for the 16th time: I'm a big fan of savory notes in mixed drinks. Spicy habanero peppers are cooled by fresh mango and that savory bite comes in by way of cilantro. These are all familiar flavors we know go well together (see: salsa), and adding tequila to the mix seemed a natural fit. The finished product should be smooth and frosty, like a slushy. If you plan on making a lot of these (and why wouldn't you!) I'd suggest making an infused syrup for greater consistency. Just put half a habanero, thinly sliced, into a saucepan with 8 oz of agave syrup. Warm to a simmer and remove from heat. Allow to cool and strain out the peppers. Add more syrup to bring the spiciness down to the level you desire.

.25 cup ripe mango (diced)

.25 cup cilantro leaves

.75 oz lime juice

.5 oz agave syrup

2 thin slices of habanero pepper

2 oz blanco tequila

Blend with ice until smooth.

Garnish with mango slice and lime wheel.

Sother Says
If you hate spicy food but love the look of this drink, skip the peppers for a sweet tropical treat.

Rosarita

1.5 oz. raspberry shrub (pg 245)

2 dashes absinthe

2 oz. blanco tequila

3 basil leaves

Shake all ingredients together with ice. Strain into an Old Fashioned glass filled with ice.

Garnish with raspberry and basil leaf.

Inspiration for cocktails can come from anywhere: Movies, songs, even salads. By way of example, this particular concoction was inspired by a salad I had, featuring basil, tarragon and raspberries with black pepper and apples. Blanco tequila has notes of citrus and cracked black pepper that pair exceptionally well with raspberries. Combine that with the anise flavor of absinthe and the fragrance of basil and you've got the makings of a great sour. But, instead of citrus, the acidic kick is being derived from vinegar in the form of a shrub. I often serve this cocktail at brunch events as it's very pretty to look at and, as it was inspired by food, it pairs well with it.

SHRUBS: WHAT'S THE DEAL?

A shrub is basically a vinegar and fruit syrup. They're extremely easy to make and virtually preserve the fruits of your choice for use when they aren't available (assuming they last that long before you use them up). I almost always use apple cider vinegar when making shrubs as it's light and fruity, but any vinegar you like will make a great one. The process is simple: Bring the vinegar and sugar to a simmer to dissolve, then remove from heat and add in the fruit. Allow to steep until cool and then purée in a blender. Some shrubs I strain and others I don't depending on the outcome I'm seeking, but as a general rule I strain any that feature seeds like raspberry, blackberry or kiwi. Pour into a sealable jar and it will keep under refrigeration for several weeks. They're a lovely addition to your cocktail arsenal but are also great as a quick refresher over ice with seltzer or sparkling wine. You can make compound shrubs also, like strawberry-jalapeño or pear-cinnamon, etc. Experiment with flavors you like and see what you come up with!

"There's naught, no doubt, so much the spirit calms as rum and true religion."

—Lord Byron

ON RUM

Nectar of pirates, power source for the tiki revolution and Papa Hemingway's spirit of choice (which is saying something), rum has a bit of a shaggy dog reputation. It plays well with fruit juice and ginger beer, but should by no means be written off as a summer-only spirit.

If you're an adventurous drinker but feel intimidated by rum, in the words of Michael Jackson, you are not alone. I am here for you. Rum is likely the most difficult spirit category to define as there are multiple producers of multiple styles and zero rules governing production. This makes for a confusing journey when trying to learn about the various types available, which makes it equally difficult to pinpoint when and how to use them.

Even the origin of the very name "rum" remains a mystery. One plausible connection suggests it originated from the last syllable of the Latin word for sugar, saccharum, as the spirit is ultimately derived from the stuff. It's also possible it chould instead be traced back to the French word *arome* for aroma or the Dutch sailors' word for a drinking glass, *roemer*. The only thing etymologists seem to agree on regarding rum is that it tastes good, and that by 1654 the name was in common use. Regardless, English style has come to be "rum," French style "rhum" and the Spanish version "ron." Each style has its own characteristics, but again, because there is no governance regarding the rules of production, it's impossible to state a concrete definition or method for creating the stuff. It's enough to drive one to drink.

It's safe to say that the spread of rum around the globe is due largely to its close association with sailing ships and their crews. Once Europeans got a taste for sugar, demand exploded, with plantations popping up all over the Caribbean. With sugar cane came a byproduct of the process of refining it, a distilled white spirit called kill devil. But because colonies were forbidden from exporting spirits, the planters found themselves with more booze than they knew what to do with. The novel solution was to sell it to Royal Navy pursers, which was a win-win for sailors as well as the colonists: The sailors got to drink, and pirate-weary island residents benefitted from the presence of armed ships in their ports. After all, pirates wanted rum too—they just didn't always pay for it. In 1687, the Royal Navy officially adopted a blend of rums from the English Caribbean islands as part of sailors' daily ration, a practice that would continue for nearly 300 years.

It's important to discuss the sugar-making process prior to discussing rum making. It takes about a year for sugarcane to reach maturity and be ready for harvest. Large machines wash the hard canes and then shred them lengthwise into ribbons. The shreds are pressed through rollers that extract all the juice. At this point, the juice tastes like mildly sweetened water. The juice is then processed with lime to clarify it, and the clarified liquid is cooked down in a vacuum to form a thick syrup. Crystals

Classic Daiquiri

The litmus test of the cocktail world: three ingredients, nowhere to hide.

.75 oz lime juice

.75 oz simple syrup

1.5 oz white rum

Shake all ingredients together with ice. Double strain into a chilled Coupe glass.

Garnish with a lime wedge.

The Hemingway

Named for Papa himself, this daiquiri variation is better than *The Old Man and the Sea.* Yeah, I said it.

.5 oz lime juice

.25 oz grapefruit juice

.25 oz Maraschino liqueur

1.5 oz white rum

Shake all ingredients together with ice. Double strain into a chilled Coupe glass.

Garnish with a grapefruit twist.

Blackbeard's Daiquiri

An iteration of my own design, this spin on the classic is rich and ruinous, like its titular pirate captain.

2 dashes Bittercube Blackstrap Bitters

.75 oz lime juice

.75 oz brown sugar syrup (pg 244)

1.5 oz dark rum

Shake all ingredients together with ice. Double strain into a chilled Coupe glass.

Garnish with a lime wheel.

of sugar are pitched in to help generate crystal formation, and finally it's spun in a centrifuge, which separates what will be sold as sugar from what can be marketed as molasses.

Neat! But also not necessarily why you bought this book. I get it. OK. Back to the booze.

Agricole-style Rhum is made by fermenting and distilling the juice of sugarcane (see why I mentioned it?). The result is a distillate that maintains the most sugarcane characteristics—a slightly sweet, green clean water. Some distillers cook the juice down to a syrup, ferment and distill it. It maintains a great deal of the cane character but is softer. Most other rum is made by fermenting and distilling molasses.

As with everything else in the rum making category, fermentation practices vary widely. Open fermentation, where ambient yeast comes into contact with the liquid in open vats is common, but so is inoculation with specific yeast strains to achieve desired results. Fermentation periods can vary as well from just a few hours to several weeks. All of these decisions are up to the maker and are chosen to achieve a desired end product.

Once distilled, half of all rums (and most Rhum Agricole) are simply bottled. The other half are aged in barrels. This is another opportunity to influence the flavor of the final product and, again, isn't regulated by any standard rules. Most of the barrels used in the aging process are bought off whisk(e)y producers, which means they'll have a char on the inside. Some rum producers use them as is, while others will re-char the barrel or scrape the char out of them altogether.

The proof of the liquid before barreling will affect how much flavor it takes on (higher proof alcohol is a better solvent and will strip more from the barrel than lower proof), but because there's no regulation on the proof at barrelling there's a wide variance in the outcomes produced by aging rums. Additionally,

the length of time a spirit ages in the barrel is up to the maker. Some rums are transferred from where they're distilled to far away ports to age in cooler climates. For instance, rums aged in the U.K. are known as Dock Rums and have a much more delicate flavor than the same spirit aged in a tropical locale. As I said: So. Many. Variables.

Splitting the various rums into families is equally daunting, so we're left to simply rely on various rules and laws set forth by the producing nations. Sadly, this means every aspect of each category can be, and likely is, different. From minimum aging, base product used, proof of the final spirit and labeling verbiage, nothing is standardized. So how are you supposed to learn what style and, more realistically, specific bottle of rum is right for you?

By drinking them of course. You can ease your way into it by using a generalized list of variations as your guide. Would you like one? OK, here goes:

The English-style rum is typically pot-distilled from molasses. This imparts a rich aromatic flavor profile that still retains much of the original molasses notes. English-style rums are often aged in oak barrels to mellow the spirit and add even more rich flavor. Consider Appleton Estate, El Dorado and Gosling's Black Seal. This style is consistently good in cocktails like the Jungle Bird and the Dark and Stormy.

Spanish-style ron is also made from fermented molasses but is typically smoother and lighter, as it's produced using continuous stills. Half of these rums are consumed young, with an equal number being aged in oak barrels to render a more complex flavor profile. Zacapa, Flor de Cana and Brugal are typical of this style. Daiquiris and the Cuba Libre were first created using Spanish-style rons.

Rhum, from France, denotes that it's a spirit made from fermented sugar cane juice rather than molasses, giving the final product an earthy and grassy aroma and flavor, as well as a sticker price that's generally higher than molasses-based rums. Rhum Clement, Rhum Neisson and Rhum Clairin are examples. Rhums are great additions to all manner of tiki-style drinks as they've got plenty of character that won't get lost even when blended with fruit juices and syrups.

One thing that seems to be universal about rum is its ability to create a community. Given the far flung reaches of the world that produce rum, it's taken on an iconic status as an exotic spirit through the introduction and resurgence of tiki culture, drawing in the adventurous and escapists alike.

The tiki movement landed on our shores in 1933 when Ernest Raymond Beaumont Gantt opened what would eventually become his ode to everything tropical, Don the Beachcomber, in Hollywood. A couple of factors were at play that helped propel the spot to instant fame. First, Americans had just come out of the shadow of Prohibition. Drinking was no longer an outlawed activity, and Americans were thirsty for a chance to imbibe out in the open again. There probably couldn't have been a better city to open such a business. Tinseltown loves to put on a show as much as its residents love to attend one. Movie stars and other members of the Hollywood

elite flocked to Don's to taste his "Rum Rhapsodies," the name he gave to his mixtures of rum, syrups and fruit juices. It's no wonder that Vic Bergeron opened his bar Trader Vic's soon after and turned it into a global chain.

By this point America was smack dab in the middle of the second World War. Americans who weren't deployed were rolling up their sleeves and pitching in where they could for the war effort (in addition to their normal jobs), and the opportunity to have a drink in a bar decorated with treasures from exotic locales was certainly a welcome respite. Returning servicemen had been exposed to cultures from all over the globe, and Don the Beachcomber was decorated to lure them in for a taste of the tropics without the foxholes.

Many of the best known rum drinks in the canon came out of just these two establishments, igniting an entire subset of cocktail culture. Scorpions, Zombies, Mai Tais and piña coladas all got their start here. Plenty of other imitators popped up across the country as the public wanted to emulate Hollywood royalty by taking in some tastes of the tiki. And it didn't just stop with drinks. Tiki was a movement. Post-modern Polynesian architecture

Malta Fizz

I was running a bar in Brooklyn and was seeking products I could use that would appeal to the neighborhood's old guard. I noticed that every bodega (corner store, for you out-of-towners) carried Malta. It's a carbonated malt beverage flavored with hops, basically a nonalcoholic beer with a rich molasses flavor, typically served over ice with condensed milk. Adding rum to the mix plays off the molasses notes, and to mimic the richness of condensed milk, I shake in an egg yolk. This drink is surprisingly rich and decadent yet maintains a dark bitter undertone. Note: No bodega cats were harmed in the procurement of this cocktail.

1 egg yolk

1 oz simple syrup

.75 oz lime juice

2 oz amber rum

2 oz Malta

Shake first 4 ingredients vigorously with ice. Strain into a glass and top with Malta.

Garnish with ground cinnamon.

began cropping up all over America, and island-inspired art was in vogue as decorations for homes throughout the U.S. As Americans were forming a wealthier middle class, even casual wear started nodding to the aesthetic. The late '50s even spawned an entire genre of music called Exotica, meant to mimic the sounds of South Pacific island nations and China. As Americans further romanticized the island lifestyle, in 1959, Hawaii became the 50th state.

As the '70s began, bars were using more and more convenience goods like canned juices, and as a result most of the authenticity that had made tiki drinks so tasty was lost. The drinks became overly sweet and heavy, leading the public to lose interest. It was the "dark ages" for cocktails in general, not just rum-fueled tiki drinks. As other vices such as LSD, cannabis and cocaine were becoming popular and more available, the once noble profession of mixology was under threat.

Luckily, the "Cocktail Renaissance" reignited a passion for cocktails and eventually resurrected tiki culture. In a quest for authenticity and knowledge, Jeff "Beachbum" Berry set out to decode the mysteries of the genre. Brother Cleve, noted musician and one of the coolest guys on the planet, traveled extensively, unearthing the sound of tiki, and it's been enjoying a revival of its own. Rum nerds have forums and sites where they share information about cocktails and rums of all manner and style. There are excellent tiki bars everywhere, as well as people who not only enjoy the drinks but actually live the lifestyle (Joe and Nicole Desmond and Adam Kolesar, I'm looking at you).

And there's one man who's made it his life's mission to amass the largest selection of rum in any one place, Martin Cate of San Fran's Smuggler's Cove. He's also one of the proprietors of Lost Lake (Chicago, IL), Hale Pele (Portland, OR) and more, where rum-driven, tiki drinks are served to hundreds of adoring fans on a daily basis.

It's this community that continues to pull together and stay engaged and curious that propelled the category out of its past and into modern times. I recommend you grab your best Hawaiian shirt and join them for a drink.

Missionary's Downfall

Famed tiki pioneer Don the Beachcomber first presented this blender favorite back in 1948. Bright with mint and rich with pineapple, honey and rum, it's a real adult frozen treat. The peach brandy is the ingredient that can cause you some issues as there aren't many on the market that aren't cloyingly sweet, so be sure to adjust the amount of honey to balance out the sweetness of your choice of brandy. Always bear in mind that drink specs are made to be tweaked to your or your guests' taste. Tinker with it 'til it's exactly to your liking. That's what Don would do.

.5 oz lime juice

.25 cup diced fresh pineapple

.25 cup mint leaves

1 oz honey syrup (pg 244)

.5 oz peach brandy

1 oz white rum

.75 cup crushed ice

Combine in a blender and blend at high-speed for 20 seconds or until smooth. Pour into your favorite glass.

Garnish with mint sprig.

LIFE

AT BEST

IS

BITTERSWEET

— JACK KIRBY

Amaro

ə'maːrəʊ / adjective

1. bitter, in Italian

noun

2. a bittersweet herbal liqueur, commonly consumed as an after-dinner digestif

3. Jr., former GM of the Philadelphia Phillies

ON AMARO

The spirits category that changed my life forever.

Amaro can be intimidating to the uninitiated. It sounds romantic in its native tongue, but the word itself translated from Italian flatly means "bitter," which conjures up feelings of ill will and curmudgeonly behavior. No one wants to be known as that bitter old man or woman. Additionally, though it's one of only five flavors we perceive, of all five flavors (salty, sweet, sour, umami/savory and bitter), only bitter is an acquired taste. Some scientists believe, when we're born we come out of the womb craving sweet. There are some solid biological reasons for this. Sweet foods are typically calorically dense and we need calories for both energy and growth. The naturally occurring sweet foods on earth are generally not poisonous, and thus pose no threat to our survival. Salt is necessary to live, and we generally like the taste upon first experience. Sour flavors shock but delight us on the first try. For proof (as well as a great laugh) search for videos of babies being fed lemon juice: the initial reaction is mostly physical but the majority delightedly go back for more. Savory foods are comforting and enjoyable right away; chicken soup is like a healing hug from a loved one.

And then there's bitter. It's a biological imperative that we perceive bitter immediately because, in general, poisons are bitter. Faster than our taste buds can relay information on whether or not we like it to our brain, our brain is setting off alarm bells saying: "This is not good for us! We are in danger! Evacuate this substance!" If children ran the world, we'd have no broccoli, dark chocolate or coffee. We wouldn't have alcohol either, as all of it is bitter to some degree. You've got to try bitter things more than once to do an end run on your hardwiring. As we get older and more experienced, we can determine the benefit of a bitter flavor and weigh it against the risk, but in general it is our only "acquired taste." And it's worth working up to.

But, let's back up a bit to where I said the brain signals for an evacuation when we taste something bitter. This is the very nature of how aperitifs and digestifs function. Though we like to categorize them separately based on when we drink them, before or after a meal, they essentially function in the same way. If you have an empty stomach and sip some Campari or a nice Negroni before lunch, the brain registers the possible threat and engages the digestive system in an effort to move the danger through the system. But, because you have an empty stomach, this process makes you feel hunger. Similarly, if you sip on an Underberg or a glass of Fernet after eating, the brain engages the system to evacuate its contents, thus helping aid in digestion. The fascinating thing here is that humans figured all of this out before having the science to back up their habits. It just felt good to drink something bitter before and after eating.

So what exactly is amaro? Great question! Unfortunately, despite being somewhat of an expert on the subject, I can't really say. Unlike other categories we've covered in this book, amaro has no rules governing its makeup. Though many Italian amaro makers would love—and are actively lobbying for—a designation of origin, they'll likely never get one because each amaro is so different. As long as it's a bitter-sweet liqueur, it pretty much qualifies as amaro. And though Italy is the undisputed king when it comes to production, bitter-sweet liqueurs cropped up all over the world somewhat simultaneously.

Herbs and botanicals have long been dried out and used in teas as medicinal elixirs. Once alcohol burst onto the scene in the form of fermented wines and beers, those elixirs were granted a longer shelf life and greater potency. The arrival of distillation further increased their longevity and strength. The addition of bitter roots, flowers or barks upped the medicinal elements of these elixirs but did so at the cost of flavor, as these ingredients often added an acrid bitterness. Savvy artisans began adding sweeteners such as honey, molasses and sugar to counter and soften the bitter taste. The stronger these blends got both in ABV and medicinal value, the more we as a species were able to venture away from home. We now had medicine that could travel without spoiling, which means in a small way, amari helped us travel the globe. As the world got smaller through commerce and trade routes, several amari began to stand out as exemplary, among them Sibilla, Meletti and Braulio. And because the public had an interest in which amari were superior, awards were generated and bestowed upon examples that had broad appeal. This practice encouraged other people to make their own amari, fueling the growth of an established market.

So how do you make an amaro? It's tough to say specifically, as nearly every maker is protective of their process. But Amaro Montenegro, perhaps because they know they've already earned a large part of the market share, has championed the notion of transparency in the industry and as such, their process is mostly available. First they chop up their bill of 40 botanicals and boil them in water for a specific period of time. Then they add alcohol to the mixture and allow it to macerate for up to 30 days. Some of this mixture is then distilled to

One of my favorite cocktail shakers, a gift from my friends at Amaro Montenegro.

become the base of the amaro, while some of it is formulated into tinctures that will be added at the end of distillation. At this stage, more alcohol is added along with water and sugar. The final, preciously guarded part of the process involves the addition of a highly concentrated distillate known as Il Premio or the Prize. It takes only one liter to flavor 15,000 bottles of Amaro Montenegro.

Another favorite amaro of mine is Jägermeister, hailing from Germany. Its base is neutral alcohol that gets macerated in "mighty oak casks" (up to 10,000 liters in capacity!) for a full year with the 56 botanicals they use to create it. Included in the list are grapefruit peel, licorice, poppy seeds, saffron and juniper berries. After a year, caramel and water are added prior to bottling. Jäger and Monte use wildly different processes for production, yet they share the same categorization; as the song sort of goes, "That's amaro."

Fans (and creators!) of the stuff can't even agree on how to serve it. Order the same amaro at any number of bars in Italy, and it'll be presented in as many different ways. Neat, chilled, on ice, with or without a slice of citrus or just a twist. It's maddening. Further, the nomenclature is equally odd: "amaro," bitter in English, refers to the darker heavier ones typically served after a meal, while "bitter," the English word, refers to lighter citrus driven ones served pre-meal. To further confuse matters, "bitters" are the little nonpotables such as Angostura or Peychaud's we use to season cocktails. It's no wonder the average consumer just throws their hands in the air and orders a vodka soda. It's also why the art of drinking for gustatory and culinary satisfaction is largely lost on the American palate. Europeans and, obviously, Italians really know how to incorporate drinking for pleasure into their mealtime habits. An aperitif before dinner in the form of a spritz while conversing and nibbling on a bowl of olives is commonplace; a cocktail on the way to the table, with varied wines served appropriately throughout the meal; a brandy with cheese after dessert followed by an amaro and possibly coffee. A leisurely affair that excites the palate by being constant only in its variability. This is how to live. Sadly, westerners skip a few of the crucial steps—especially the aperitif and digestif—typically because they're foreign to them. They lack the knowledge base to feel comfortable ordering these weird bottles of bitter booze. The only way to gain that knowledge is through experimentation, which means occasionally drinking something that'll trigger that "evacuate!" signal in your brain. Just remember, you've overcome it before.

In this way, amari are a lot like wine. You can read as much as you like, but that'll never compare to actually smelling and tasting what's in the bottle. Thankfully, familiarizing yourself with amaro is less of a constant endeavor because unlike wine, once you understand what each maker is doing and what their expressions taste like, they won't change year over year. Amari makers pride themselves on strict adherence to their 100-plus-year-old recipes, another way in which they're unique. Further, it

What Makes an Amaro...

Because each amaro is made using a proprietary recipe and even proprietary techniques, I can't precisely say "Amaro is basically just vodka infused with bitter stuff and some sweeteners," which is a shame, as I'm pretty sure you were starting to fall in love with that presentation. But I can generalize and say amaro is based on a simple, four-pronged approach:

Alcohol

Some form of booze is always the base, typically a spirit of the maker's choosing that's usually mild in flavor—neutral grain spirits or high-proof vodka (see?)—though some use whisk(e)y, rum or even mezcal depending on what they want the profile of the final product to be.

Bittering Agent

These ingredients (various roots, barks, flowers, seeds and nuts) are added to lend a bitter flavor to the mixture. The maker can use as many or as few of these as they choose—it's their recipe after all.

Flavoring Agent

The purpose of these ingredients is, you guessed it, to add flavor. Citrus peels, flowers, anise, menthol and more are added in various doses depending on the desired outcome.

Sweetener

These ingredients, including molasses, beet molasses, sugar or honey, are added to sweeten and balance the bitterness, which is to say, to make these potent potables palatable.

As long as all four components are present, it's probably an amaro, especially if the maker is deliberately trying to produce something bitter. I'd be remiss if I didn't point out that based on the knowledge that amaro is made up of alcohol, bittering agents, sweeteners and water that it qualifies as the definition of an Old Fashioned: spirit, bitters, sugar and water. All amari are bottled Old Fashioneds. Cheers to that!

pays to be adventurous. If you're the type who'll risk $25 or more on a meal comprised of ingredients you've never heard of, why wouldn't you risk $8 or so on trying an ounce of amaro?

Because I brought it up, food is also a helpful analogue for my relationship with amari. All amari have savory qualities and, since I spent nearly a dozen years cooking with savory components, I feel particularly drawn to that style beverage. When I first stepped behind a bar, I was wide eyed and excited. I dove into every aspect of the cocktail world and applied my skills as a researcher to this new-to-me field. I devoured books, scoured the internet, frequented all manner of bars and seminars. I started making my own grenadine and orgeat; my own ginger beer and triple sec. I applied my culinary skills to the liquid world in a methodical way, and as I moved forward I constantly found myself gravitating toward stirred boozy drinks. First I was enthralled by bitters, then I found amari, complex bottles of balance and texture, ready to enjoy. I began incorporating them into my programs and stacking as many as I could find in my back bar. Then, as luck would have it, I was asked to join a small team at a pop-up bar devoted to all things amaro and bitter. I leapt at the chance. We became a permanent fixture, I left my other jobs and took it on full force. At first, we had no real aspirations beyond just having a good time and showing off unique things that we loved, but now we're a mecca for the bitter obsessed; a place where you can explore a category with people who truly care about it. I've often said, "There's no better place to get an education than at a bar" and if my bar is anything, it's a school where you can drink.

In my 240 square feet of pure awesome, Amor y Amargo, I get to taste and talk about amari and bitters for around 50 hours a week. Frankly, I feel lucky that the category is so varied and confusing. If it were all set in stone, I'd've run out of things to say and explore long ago. This category keeps me challenged. The patrons keep coming at me

with questions, and often we have to use collective cognition to surmise the answers together. As we've created a bit more demand, more supply has been made available. When we opened, we didn't have enough bottles to fill the shelves. As creators from around the globe started sending me new bottles to experiment with, I had to build more shelves. Today, they're overflowing. I rotate stock on and off the back bar every few weeks so unseen bottles will get some time in the limelight. "What's that?" "When did you get it?" "What does it taste like?" Well here's a glass...let's find out.

Amor y Amargo has the largest selection of both tincture bitters and amari in New York City and is among the largest collections in the world. Building the beverage program there has been a journey that's allowed me to travel internationally to speak about the category to eager crowds of bartenders and consumers alike. Every day I learn something, and every day I share what I've learned with whomever wants to hear it. I've met the makers, distillers, herbalists and blenders of all manner of amari, and many have welcomed me behind the curtain. I champion the category as a whole rather than glomming on to a particular brand. In that way, I'm like Dr. Seuss's Lorax—I speak for the trees. I'm lucky, and I know it.

But I also worked hard. And saying that is OK. Because by consigning my success specifically to luck would be ignoring all the research, studying, traveling and tireless tinkering I did to put myself in the position of landing a dream job. I may be uniquely suited to stand behind the tiled bar at Amor y Amargo, but my work ethic and dedication to learning more isn't unique to my job. You can apply it to anything you care about—and you should. And when you find yourself making a living doing whatever it is you want to do, savor the reward of that blessing. Then come to New York, visit me at my little bar on East 6th Street and let me pour you a well-deserved drink. It might taste bitter, but it'll also be sweet.

Youthful Expression

2 dashes Bittercube Cherry
Bark Vanilla Bitters

1 oz Ramazzotti

1 oz Bourbon

1 oz London Dry gin

Seltzer

Combine first 4 ingredients in a
Collins glass. Add ice and gently stir
to chill. Pour seltzer down the spiral
of a bar spoon to fill.

No garnish.

Ramazzotti is a Kola Nut amaro packed with dried fruit flavors that's reminiscent of Dr Pepper. When combined with bourbon's subtle orange spine and the herbal notes of London Dry gin, this cocktail is a playful riff reminiscent of the Cuba Libre. The cherry bark vanilla bitters and seltzer give a lift to the drink and make it seem far less dangerous than it actually is. This is the type of drink that, though it's sophisticated in flavor, hearkens back to a simpler approach to drinking—even if that approach ends in a competition to see how many you can down in an afternoon.

A LOVIN' SPOONFUL

There is no tool in the bartender's kit as simple and useful as the spiral bar spoon. It's been kicking around since the early days of mixology and is as indispensable as it is humble. Like a good chef's knife, after several hours of use, it becomes an extension of the user's hand and wielded correctly it looks like an orchestra conductor's baton or a magician's wand. They come in myriad styles and lengths and are often adorned on one end by icons of the genre like pineapples, skulls or, more practically, a small fork for grabbing garnishes (or threatening greedy hands that wander too close to your garnish assortment—it's not a salad bar, Courtney!). Choose one that's sturdy but lightweight, as a heavy one can wear out your wrist after prolonged use. Once you've selected your spoon, measure the capacity of its bowl. They're generally not standardized but once you know its capacity you can employ it as a device to measure elements of your own design. If your spoon has good balance, it's also easy to gain torque when using it to crack ice. Holding the target in the palm of your nondominant hand, and holding the spoon at near the top in your other hand, gently but firmly strike the ice with the back of the bowl.

Another vital feature is the spoon's coiled stem, which helps the spoon glide easily in your fingers as you stir drinks. As an added bonus, if you're making a drink that's "topped with seltzer" or any other carbonated beverage, pouring the liquid down the spoon while it's inserted to the bottom of the glass will result in a better integration of effervescence into the drink. It's physics! I choose Cocktail Kingdom 30 cm teardrop spoons as my weapon of choice. The bowl measures approximately 2.5 mL, the spiral is tight and comfortable, and the spoon itself is lightweight, beautiful and built to last.

SPOTLIGHT ON
AMARO MONTENEGRO

GROCERIES FOR THE QUEEN

Peter Heering was a grocery clerk in Copenhagen when he first began production of his eponymous cherry liqueur in 1818. Much further along in time, in 1885 Stanislao Cobianchi created his elixir, with a huge nose of orange and orange blossoms tempered by bitter agents like Artemesia and marjoram, in tribute to his queen. The body is light and reminiscent of cucumber and celery juices. Cherry and orange are a natural match and chocolate is a match for each of them as well. Combining these two historic potables in one cocktail creates a lush, juicy effect that's evocative of orange blossoms and dark cherry. Combined with light-bodied gin and accented by the chocolate bitters, the Montenegro becomes the star of the show in a cocktail fit for royalty.

....

2 dashes Scrappy's
Chocolate Bitters
....
.75 oz orange juice
....
.75 oz Amaro Montenegro
....
1 oz Cherry Heering
....
1.5 oz London Dry gin
....

Whip shake with a few pebbles of ice to chill and aerate. Pour into a glass filled with pebble ice. Top with more pebble ice.

Garnish with luxardo cherries and orange twist.

In the late 1800s, a young man named Stanislao Cobianchi was set to attend seminary and live a life of the cloth but had a last-minute change of heart. A bit of a rebel who was fond of adventure, he set out to explore the world against his family's will. Through his many travels as well as his interest in botany, he gained knowledge of a wide variety of herbs, spices and botanicals. When he returned to Italy in 1885, he founded a liqueur company in Bologna, later naming it after Princess Elena of Montenegro after she married Victor Emmanuel to become Queen of Italy. A romantic tribute, it was also a deft marketing tactic. At the turn of the century as now, everybody loves a celebrity. The queen's namesake amaro boasts a blend of 40 botanical ingredients from all over the globe. Only three people are privy to the full recipe.

Today, Amaro Montenegro is the bestselling amaro in Italy, a testament to its appeal. When visiting the country you'll see it on nearly every back bar and at many cafés. It's as prevalent as Jack Daniels is in the States, and for good reason: Simply put, it's delicious. The aroma is enticing with hints of sweet orange oil and vanilla, and the flavors are familiar; citrusy bright orange peel coupled with warming spice from clove, cinnamon and nutmeg. It's also got a pleasing ABV of only 23%, meaning its kick is mild but not unnoticeable. It's an amaro that can be consumed at any time for any occasion. It's also a favorite to reach for when introducing someone to the category of amari as its bitterness is subtle enough to be inoffensive even to the most untrained palate. I literally can't recall a single instance of pouring it for a first timer and having them balk.

It's also adored by bartenders for its ease of use and versatility. Its lighter body gives it an almost juice-like quality, allowing it to stand in for some or all of the juice in a cocktail. Try using it to replace the lime juice in your next Margarita; the result is a silkier, less tart variation with pleasing herbal qualities that blend brilliantly with blanco tequila. Citrus, cinnamon and vanilla are right at home with rum and pebble ice so I often sneak a little Monte into tiki drinks. It also carries enough sweetness to take the position of modifying liqueurs. Let it tag in for the Benedictine in a Vieux Carré (pg 214) for a more citrus-forward bend on the stirred classic, or replace the Maraschino liqueur in your next Hemingway Daiquiri (pg 174) for an added layer of complexity and citrus. Due to its relatively low ABV, it's also at home playing the role of vermouth in cocktails, both sweet or dry. A Manhattan (pg 74) or Martini (pg 30) with Montenegro will delight and surprise your guests. The House shot at Amor y Amargo is a 50/50 of Montenegro and blanco tequila with grapefruit bitters called "The Full Monte."

Just the Paperwork

There's something calming about creating a routine to end the chaos of a bar shift. For a long stretch of time, this cocktail was part of mine. I'd drink this scaffa (a room temperature cocktail) every night as I was closing the bar and doing the paperwork. There's a thread that runs through the components of the cocktail: Cognac, Amaro Nonino and Cocchi Americano are all made from grapes. The resulting cocktail has a medium body and a really juicy flavor profile, but again, there's no juice in sight. The orange bitters and the twist create an aroma that'll further enforce the fresh-squeezed illusion. Now, back to the books.

.5 oz water

2 dashes orange bitters

1 oz Cocchi Americano

1 oz Cognac

1.5 oz Amaro Nonino

Build in a Rocks glass, and serve neat.

Garnish with an orange twist.

EXPLORING THE SCAFFA

This all but forgotten category of cocktails is served neat, always without chilling and often without any dilution. Scaffas are spiritus drinks that don't feature any juice but may be constructed with sugar or syrups. If, like me, you prefer your spirits and other potables served neat, this style will make perfect sense to you. Scaffas likely sprang up during a time when ice was scarce and therefore expensive. The word itself is an Italian term for cupboard or cabinet and may refer to making drinks with whatever you have in the pantry. While there aren't many examples to be found, the category is making a comeback at tiny cocktail bars all over the world. They're also well-suited for your pocket flask for those times when ice is nowhere to be found.

FERNET-BRANCA

ODD BEDFELLOWS

At first glance this drink seems out of character for its main boozy component. However, the mentholated Branca is tamed by the cacao and rich coconut cream to create a cocktail that's not too far removed from the venerable piña colada. The additional chocolate notes from the cacao combine with the Branca to evoke a York Peppermint Patty. The result is a bracing, breathtaking cocktail that strikes a lot of familiar notes. The overproof rum comes creeping in to lay down a funky baseline but doesn't overpower the true nature of this playful tipple. It's proof positive that Fernet is equally welcome whether you're listening to a three-piece band in a smoky Italian cocktail den or nodding off to a steel drummer playing over the waves on the beach in Miami.

....

1 oz coconut cream

....

1.5 oz pineapple juice

....

.25 oz Smith and Cross
Jamaican Rum

....

.5 oz creme de cacao

....

.75 oz El Dorado 8-Year-Old Rum

....

1 oz Fernet-Branca

....

Whip shake with a few pebbles of ice to chill and aerate. Pour into a glass filled with pebble ice. Top with more pebble ice.

Garnish with a pineapple wedge and/or mint sprigs. Add grated bitter chocolate if you've got some.

Fernet is a subcategory of the overall umbrella of amaro. However, and quite frustratingly, there are no rules or governance that outline what exactly makes something a Fernet. There are some commonalities that seem to bundle the various brands together, though loosely, and the list of botanicals gives us at least a clue if not an outright indicator. Aloe, specifically black aloe ferox, is common as it adds bitterness as well as the deep dark color associated with the subcategory. Additionally, rhubarb and menthol are common, though I can name at least one label that has no discernible mintiness. Saffron is also a common thread (Fernet-Branca claims to purchase up to 75% of the world's supply each year). Beyond this loose list of potential connections, Fernets tend to be higher in ABV than other amari and are also typically more aggressively bitter. As amaro already lacks any overarching rules, why not toss in a subcategory that has none either?

Fernet-Branca, founded in 1845, is the overwhelming titan of the subcategory, and it achieved its monolithic status through a combination of ingenuity and good fortune. Prohibition actually helped solidify its seat of power in the United States. With only a few slight alterations to the formula, it continued to be sold legally in the States as a medicinal spirit. When Prohibition ended, they were in a great position to start an advertising campaign faster than most other spirits makers. They also employed talented artists for poster and print ads as well as offered branded materials like ashtrays and glassware to increase brand awareness. It worked.

There are 27 botanicals listed as being included in Fernet-Branca but, as usual, very few people have access to the full recipe. Only the chairman of the company can see how the puzzle pieces come together. Several that are known include aloe, saffron, chamomile and bitter orange, and others that can be surmised include ginger, cinchona, menthol and rhubarb. The result is a cast-iron black elixir that packs a punch of 39% ABV. Sharply bitter with a cooling hit of mint that fills the nose and soothes the tongue, it still has enough sweetness (possibly from beet molasses) to bring it back into balance.

As it's such a unique and powerful flavor, it tends to annihilate the other components in a cocktail unless poured with a judicious hand. Start with classics like the Hanky Panky (pg 227) or the Toronto, then slip a spoonful into other cocktails to test the waters. You can ramp up the amount by stacking it against items of similar weight and viscosity such as cream or pineapple juice. It's a fun addition to tiki drinks as it's a total surprise to the drinker when you reveal the "secret." In San Francisco, where a quarter of Italy's production of Branca is consumed, they shoot it with a ginger ale or ginger beer chaser in what's known as the Bartender's Handshake. Fernet-Branca is also enjoyed by industry professionals in a 50/50 shot with Campari called—what else?—the Ferrari.

Braulio-Cano

Though it's produced in Italy, flavor-wise I associate Braulio with the Swiss Alps (Valtellina, the town Braulio hails from, is nestled along the Italian border with Switzerland). Laced with soft flavors of pine and bitter mountain herbs, it also has elegant layers of berries, citrus and caramel. Cocchi Rosa is a Rosé aperitif wine that's lush and juicy with hints of bitter strawberry—sort of like your favorite sangria mixed with the texture of sweet vermouth. Combining these two in equal measure with seltzer results in a low ABV riff on the Americano that's bright and refreshing. The addition of orange citrate gives it a final lift of fresh orange fragrance. We served this on tap at the bar one summer and couldn't make it fast enough. On a hot day it's also improved greatly by a small scoop of vanilla ice cream!

2 dashes Bittermens Orange Citrate

1.5 oz Braulio

1.5 oz Cocchi Rosa

Seltzer

Build in a Highball. Add ice and stir to chill. Pour seltzer down the spiral of a bar spoon to fill.

Garnish with an orange.

THE AMERICANO

Originally called the Milano-Torino in reference to the birthplaces of its key components (Campari and sweet vermouth), it later became known as the Americano because of its popularity among tourists visiting from the States. Originally crafted by Gaspare Campari—the creator of Campari—at his bar Café Campari in the 1860s, it's been a staple of the Italian drinking landscape ever since. It's a harmonious balance of bitter and sweet lengthened with a burst of bubbles from the seltzer. The café, located in the center of Milan, still exists, and is a bustling spot filled with all manner of people enjoying the bar's most famous drink. If you find yourself in Milan, it's a must visit for the view and people watching alone. Notably, the Americano is the precursor to the Negroni, which substitutes London Dry gin for the seltzer for a more bracing, if still absolutely refreshing, cocktail.

Oh My Word!

This variation of the Last Word forgoes the lime juice in favor of the juice-like quality of Amaro Montenegro fortified with lime bitters. It employs Old Tom gin instead of the traditional London Dry to bring down the intensity, primarily because as a stirred cocktail, it won't benefit from the aeration caused by shaking it. The result is a more spirit-forward version of a classic that still harkens back to the notes of original. Herbal, sweet and pungent with a less tart effect than the Last Word, all the components are also shelf stable, meaning you can mix up a whole bottle of it to have on hand at a moment's notice.

2 dashes orange bitters

.75 oz Maraschino liqueur

.75 oz green Chartreuse

.75 oz Amaro Montenegro

.75 oz Old Tom gin

Stir with plenty of ice to chill and dilute. Strain and serve up.

No garnish.

SPOTLIGHT ON
MELETTI

Founded by Silvio Meletti in 1870 in Ascoli Piceno, a town in Le Marche region of Italy, Meletti's location has as much to do with its success as anything else. Neatly tucked in a river valley between the Apennine Mountain range and the Adriatic Sea, Ascoli Piceno offers ample access to mountainous herbs, and its proximity to the rivers, as well as the fact that the town was along the Via Salaria, or "salt road," afforded it ample access to trade routes. It's an ideal place to launch a liqueur company.

The Meletti family has been producing spiritus potables since the late 1800s. Most well-known is their award-winning anisette (made with anise seeds using a cold extraction technique pioneered by Silvio), but they also produce a delicious red bitter as well as an incomparable amaro that bears the family name. Meletti Amaro is bittered with Gentian, but also includes other floral notes from violet flowers and saffron. It also features cloves, anise seeds and bitter orange peel. Though they won't divulge their full ingredient list, we can also surmise that kola nut, from which Coca-Cola, Pepsi and other colas once derived their signature flavor, is a key component of Meletti. It gives the amaro a leathery quality that's backed up with flavors of cocoa and baking spices. Because it carries such a familiar flavor profile to America's beloved soft-drink, it's an amaro that's easy to sell a person on.

To that end, a jumping off point for drinking Meletti is to simply pour it into a Collins glass with ice and charge it with seltzer. A squeeze from a lemon wedge really helps play up the cola notion. It's fun to give it this treatment with your favorite "something and Coke" for a more complex and boozy variation: Meletti clocks in at 32% ABV, so it's no slouch. Further, I typically reach for the bottle when I want to add herbal notes accompanied by a richness of body and a slightly bittersweet finish. It enhances spirits simply split 50/50, neat as a quick shot or over ice like an Old Fashioned. I particularly enjoy it with spicy Rittenhouse Rye in a 50/50 shot called the Jimbo, named after NYC bartender Jimmy Palumbo who made the shot out of necessity during a snowstorm. All he had on hand were the two components and, in an effort to make them last a little longer, combined them to delicious results. He was known to serve them in unused shotgun shells at one point. Ah, memories.

As I often suggest with amari, during your experimentation phase, start by substituting it for some or all of a tertiary modifier. Drop out the Cointreau for Meletti for a radical twist on a Man o' War. Or, try a rum-based Negroni (pg 37) with Meletti instead of Campari for a deeper, island-spiced variation on the classic.

SOMETHING LIKE IT

Most amari makers recommend drinking their product neat, on the rocks or with seltzer. I typically take those approaches when first getting to know a new (to me) amaro, and usually in that order. I want to taste it as the maker gave it to me, straight from the bottle. Then I try it over ice to see what a little dilution does to change the flavor, and finally, I'll lengthen it with seltzer. The effervescence lets the amaro dance over my tongue and the aromas fill my olfactory senses.

As a Kola Nut amaro, Meletti tasted very much like a fountain cola when served with sparkling water, and it seemed a natural fit to try it as a substitute for Coke Classic in a riff on the Cuba Libre. This cocktail uses a white rum in concert with lime juice and lime bitters, the small amount of gin heightens the herbal qualities of the amaro and, with the addition of seltzer, comes off as the real deal; or at least "Something like it."

....
2 dashes Scrappy's Lime Bitters
....
.25 oz lime juice
....
.5 oz London Dry gin
....
1 oz white rum
....
1.5 oz Meletti amaro
....
Seltzer
....

Build in a Collins glass. Add ice. Top with seltzer.

Garnish with a lime wedge.

Kola Sour

I have a lot of fun working unexpected ingredients together in ways that are tasty and a little surprising to my guests. Don't get me wrong, my guests aren't guinea pigs—I do my homework, and in this case my homework is drinking. Towing the line between an egg sour and a Mai Tai variation, this cocktail came to be during one such study session. The soft cola and bitter orange notes from the Meletti cozy up to the sweet almond orgeat while the lemon keeps the balance between tart and sweet. The clean white rum provides the backbone and egg white generates a fluffy texture that makes the drink attractive to look at as well as delightfully light on the palate.

The resulting flavors are not unlike a rum and cherry coke, but instead of fizzy it's fluffy. Orgeat has a distinctly marzipan flavor, which tastes similar to the compounds found in cherry pits. The bitters offer an aroma of cherry and vanilla on top that reinforce this notion. It's one homework assignment I'm happy to turn in.

1 Dash Bittercube Vanilla Cherry Bark Bitters

1 small egg white

.75 oz lemon juice

.5 oz orgeat (pg 246)

1 oz Meletti amaro

1 oz Banks 5 Island Rum

Dry shake first five ingredients to emulsify, then add ice. Shake to combine. Strain into a Rocks glass of fresh ice. Optional: Paint with drops of cherry bitters.

No garnish.

CARING FOR CARAMEL

When you read "caramel coloring" on an ingredient label, your first instinct may be to turn your nose up at the notion of an artificial chemical being added to whatever it is you were about to enjoy. As a result, people often think of caramel coloring in a negative light. Though you typically won't find caramel coloring (or any other ingredients) on the side of an amaro label, it's nevertheless an integral part of what makes many of them—including Meletti—so damn delicious. It's maligned because it's misunderstood. For starters, caramel coloring isn't made artificially. It's a natural process: you simply reduce sugar and water down until the sugar goes well past the caramel stage and literally turns black.

As a flavor additive it's often essential to amari (as well as colas and the like). An easily understood fact, given that it's made from sugar and water is that it adds sweetness. But because it's sugar that's been burned to black, it also adds bitterness—burning sugars, or anything really, brings about bitter flavors. The dark burnt color helps to tint the final product, and the overall viscosity of the caramel helps create a more luscious texture.

As a young man, Girolamo Varnelli lived in the heart of the Sibillini Mountains where he studied the plant life and vegetation. This mountainous area, located in Le Marche region of Italy, is so pristine and beautiful that it was converted into a national park to preserve its diversity and splendor. Young Girolamo's interests led to his being recognized as a superior herbalist, and in 1868 he founded his namesake business. At first he developed a tonic with anti-fever and antimalarial properties called Amaro Sibilla, which he named after a legendary fortune teller of the region. With sharp gentian and quinine notes wrapped in a dark lush herbal base, it remains among my favorite amari today. After achieving great success with this first elixir he went on to produce a wildly popular dry anisette and then Amaro Dell'erborista. The company now boasts a line of herbal liqueurs at least 13 labels strong, but the first three remain the mainstays of the brand.

Dell'erborista is a blend of gentian and mountain herbs along with cinnamon, clove, rhubarb, cinchona bark and citrus peels. There are a few markers that make this amaro stand out. First, the herbs and roots used are toasted using a wood fire. Next, a local apiary provides the honey to sweeten the mixture. Finally, after resting in barrels for seven months, it's bottled without the mid step of filtration. The appearance is a pale yellowish-brown that's slightly murky, not dissimilar to a wheat beer. All summed up, it's a sharply bitter yet still light-on-the-palate amaro that tastes of lightly smoked tea and bitter honey with a prickly tannic quality that dries the tongue. In my mind, it could be shelved alongside a lapsang souchong tea.

I highly recommend drinking this amaro neat prior to experimenting with it in cocktails. Its light aroma can fool you into thinking it's harmless, but the flavor is aggressive and can overpower other ingredients. Once you've got a handle on how to tame and employ the amaro, go with complementary flavors like citrus, smoke and honey. Substitute it for some of the lemon juice in a Penicillin cocktail for an even smokier version with a bitter bite. Or try it with a malty Genever and a dry vermouth for a white Negroni (pg 37) variation. Shaken into a classic Bees Knees (pg 51) will turn it from a sweet honied cocktail into a snappy, complex bitter version. On cold nights by the fire I sip it mixed half and half with a blended scotch. On cold nights behind the bar, I shoot it with friends blended in equal parts with a smoky, peated scotch. It's also perfectly at home in hot cocktails like my Herbalist Tea.

HERBALIST TEA

Amaro Dell'erborista is a honey-sweetened gentian and herbal bitter. They procure the honey from a local apiary where the bees are pollinating the very same botanicals that are in the amaro. The honey takes on a bitterness of its own in the same way that blueberry honey takes on the flavor of the fruit. Varnelli also fire roasts the botanicals prior to maceration, giving the final product a slightly smoky nuance. I find that it's a natural accompaniment to hot tea. Adding a bold peated scotch along with the spicy zing of ginger makes it feel almost therapeutic. The final aromatic note comes from cloves studded into a fresh lemon wedge.

....

2 dashes 18.21 Lemon Ginger Tincture

....

2 oz piping hot water

....

.25 oz ginger syrup (pg 244)

....

.25 oz lemon juice

....

.5 oz peated Scotch whisky (I use Laphroaig)

....

1.5 oz Dell'erborista

....

Add all ingredients to a warmed mug.

Garnish with clove-studded lemon wedge.

ALCOHOL MAY BE MAN'S WORST ENEMY BUT THE BIBLE SAYS LOVE YOUR ENEMY

— FRANK SINATRA

Mixed Libations

mikst li'bāSHəns// / noun

1. in this case, a cocktail containing equal portions of two or more kinds of liquor

2. various offerings to the gods

3. a great name for a Beach Boys-themed cocktail bar

ON MIXED LIBATIONS

Like all the other sections, but poured in one glass.

Mixology is an entirely American invention. It's taking a bunch of things you like and adding them together—one of the basic notions of our country since its inception. We piled all these different people and cultures into one place, and all the various traditions and habits and weird tics they brought with them sort of fell into what you likely remember from your first civics class as the Crèvecœurian Melting Pot. Mixology is the same—we just use a mixing glass. We take one thing we like, mix it with another thing we like, add a couple dashes of a few other things we like and hopefully come away with something we love. Generally, that's not how most of the spirits I've detailed in this volume were originally intended to be consumed. Most distillers don't create a product to an exact specification with a desired flavor profile, in some cases centuries old, with the hope that it'll be shaken or stirred as a minor component in a major American cocktail. Most spirits were intended to be served on their own, as they are. A common question I receive when customers encounter all the amaro I have on offer at the bar is "So what do I do with it?" You drink it. That's why they made it. What they really mean, of course, is "What should I mix it with?" And the truth is, you shouldn't technically mix them with anything. That's not why they were originally created. People drink them on their own all over the world—we're the weird ones who

want to mix them with stuff. And yet, an entire industry of which I am a part has grown out of this wrongheaded idea. Which means those of us who are wrong might well be onto something.

So how best to determine which spirits will work in harmony with one another? To answer the question let's start with an example of a classic that engages in this sort of rule-breaking to great success: the Vieux Carré (pg 214). This 1930s throwback in the cocktail canon was first conceived at the bar in the lobby of a grand New Orleans lodging known as the Hotel Monteleone. The Monteleone is considered the gateway to the French quarter, and barkeep Walter Bergeron borrowed the colonial name for the area to title his tipple.

It combines, in equal measure, the all-American spirit rye whiskey and the then very popular Cognac. Rye whiskey is relatively thin on the palate and boasts a slightly fruity but distinctively spicy flavor. It's also quite dry and even more so as you get into higher proof expressions. Cognac has the ability to taste like tea, flowers, cocoa, leather, cigars, vanilla and even black truffle (though typically not all these flavors are present in a single bottle). Being a mixed drink, it's likely the Vieux Carré would employ a simpler Cognac with notes of cocoa and vanilla—a grape distillate that's aged in oak, it's typically more lush on the tongue. The Vieux Carré goes on to add an equal measure of sweet vermouth (likely to tame the heat of the spirits) and fortifies this Manhattan riff with a small

The Suffering Bastard in a less charming glass than its tiki mug on pg 207.

and upon hearing them complain of hangovers, Joe set about creating a "cure." The Suffering Bastard is a buck consisting of 1 oz gin (likely London Dry), 1 oz bourbon, .75 oz lime juice and 2 dashes of Angostura bitters all topped with ginger beer. A crisp refresher that packs a punch. Why does it work? Bourbon has a full texture on the tongue and bursts with caramel and vanilla notes. It's also got plenty of oak and hints of citrus, especially orange. London Dry gin is packed with herbal flavors like angelica, coriander and citrus peels dominated by juniper. At first glance, this doesn't sound like a match made in heaven. But, as you consider the cocktail's other components, you can start to draw a Venn diagram where the characteristics begin to overlap in a complementary way. Lime juice is a common sidekick to gin, in cocktails such as the Gimlet or the Southside, while lime juice and bourbon are commonly coupled in drinks like a Rickey or a Derby. It's pretty common for ginger to be paired with both as well—think about the Gin Mule and the Presbyterian. So, whereas the Vieux Carré used spirits that mesh well, in this drink the spirits are less complementary, but the additional ingredients act as a bridge bringing them together.

The practice of mixing spirits can also be examined through another famous highball, the Cuba Libre. It's origins are uncertain but it can be traced back at least to 1900 when Coca-Cola was first distributed to the tiny island nation of Cuba. Early recipes for the drink call for not only light rum but also gin. The herbal quality of gin accentuates the baking spice and vanilla notes of the cola. The original call, Bacardi light rum, has delicate citrus, umami and almond flavors that balance the citrus tang of fresh lime juice. The culmination is far superior to a rum and coke (commonly mistaken to be the Cuba Libre). Oh, how the mighty fall at the hands of the lazy! I'm not here to say that rum and coke

amount of Bénédictine, a sweet herbal liqueur, and finally seasons it up with dashes of both Angostura and New Orleans's own Peychaud's Bitters. Combining spicy and fruity notes with rich cocoa and vanilla seems pretty logical when it's broken down in such a way (some of the best chocolates in a Whitman's sampler engage in similar flavor fusion), and the cocktail has lived this long because of how well these spirits play together.

Another classic example of a split-based cocktail is considerably more simple: The Suffering Bastard. Chemist Joe Scialom created the drink in Cairo at the famed Shepheard's Hotel in 1942. The hotel was frequented by British soldiers at the time isn't delicious, I'm just here to set the record straight that it is most certainly not a Cuba Libre without at least the addition of lime juice (not just a lime wedge) and that it can be vastly improved with the addition of a crisp London dry Gin to fortify it further.

Let's consider a few modern cocktails included in this section. Rough Seas (pg 217), a cocktail of my own design, tackles a less likely pairing, that of Jägermeister and cachaça. Jägermeister is a kräuterlikör (herbal liqueur) made by the Mast family in Wolfenbüttel, Germany, since 1935. It boasts a botanical bill of 56 ingredients and, at a proof of 70, is adding punch as well as flavor. The most forward notes of Jäger include star anise, cinnamon, grapefruit and ginger. Dating back to 1532, cachaça is a fermented sugar cane juice distillate from Brazil that predates rum by nearly 300 years. The aroma and subsequently the flavor is reminiscent of cut grass and briny olives. Cachaça is the spirit of choice in the national drink of Brazil, the caipirinha, which consists of the spirit and sugar muddled with lime.

The Rough Seas reins in all these flavors by taking them down a path of tiki inspiration. Bursts of star anise and cinnamon from Jägermeister pair well with the orgeat and ginger syrup while the funky cachaça is tempered by tart lemon juice. The amalgam is aerated and served over a mountain of pebble ice resulting in a cocktail that is far greater than the sum of its individual parts.

Another of the original recipes herein, my friend Chris Elford created the Sharpie Mustache (pg 219) during his tenure at Amor y Amargo. In what we refer to as a Zen cocktail, meaning that all major components exist in equal parts, it combines rye, London Dry gin, Meletti (a Kola Nut amaro) and Bonal (a Gentian and quinine-wine based aperitif). A few dashes of tiki bitters that have ginger, nutmeg and mace in them and you've got what, on paper, is an unlikely combination. But, if we break it all down, we can easily see that the assertive spice of rye pairs beautifully with the herbal nature of the gin. I don't think anyone would argue with using both herbs and spices when they cook—which to me suggests they can work together in a glass as well. Meletti tastes of cola; it's got hints of citrus, leather and vanilla. (I've often said that if Coca-Cola were flat, less sweet and alcoholic, it'd be the bestselling amaro on earth). Whiskey and Coke is a commonly ordered highball that's rich and spicy, and gin and coke is its less common, refreshing counterpart. The snappy dryness of Bonal serves as the "vermouth" in this "Negroni"-style cocktail (bearing in mind that a Negroni-style cocktail is spirit, vermouth, amaro and bitters).

The Rough Seas

Some spirit combinations that I've come to rely on and what they yield when piecing together new offerings include...

Rhum Agricole and Peated Scotch

Rhum Agricole is a pungent and fragrant cane juice rum distilled in pot stills. It has a sulfurous "funk" in its aroma commonly called hogo. This gives the rhum an umami and vegetal aroma and flavor. Expressions from Martinique also clock in at 140 proof, so the heat is on too! Peated scotch is whisky made from malt that has been dried over a peat-fueled fire, effectively smoking the malt. That aroma and flavor carry through the distilling process. When these two spirits are blended together, the result is a smoky and savory flavor bomb that can transform a cocktail from passé to remarkable.

Rum and Mezcal

Similarly, an aged Jamaican rum like Appleton Estate VX tastes of fermented fruit and molasses with aromas of citrus peel and banana. Mezcal is a product of multiple varieties of the agave plant, but prior to fermentation, it's cooked, resulting in smoky flavors in the final distillate. When the two are combined, the resulting flavor is similar to that of grilled bananas. Savory and sweet battle for position and with small adjustments to ratio you can control which comes out on top.

White Rum and Genever

White rums have flavors of citrus, mushroom and almonds. Genever is malty and sweet with herbs and juniper. Blending the two results in a savory and funky combination that pairs well with herbal liqueurs like Chartreuse and Genepy.

Whiskey and Whisky

Bourbon, by law, must contain at least 51% corn in its mashbill. Corn is a very sweet grain—it's the source of corn syrup, the most consumed sweetener on Earth! So, bourbon has an inherently sweet flavor in addition to caramel notes and hints of oak and orange. Conversely, rye must contain at least 51% rye grains. These grains result in a drier and spicier distillate. Peated scotch is smoky and earthy. In the Campfire Old Fashioned (pg. TK) we combine all three to find harmony between sweet, spice and smoke. In short, not all whisk(e)y tastes the same—you can balance and enhance the different notes in each by blending them together.

Blanco Tequila and Mezcal

Tequila is a product of specifically the blue agave produced in Jalisco. Tequila has a vegetal flavor with aromas of white pepper, citrus and herbs like cilantro. These flavors are a natural to pair with the smokey vegetal flavors and aromas from mezcal. This is a great way to ensure you're getting plenty of mileage from your mezcal as they're often overpowering in cocktails unless tempered.

Apple Brandy and Reposado Tequila

Apple brandy has obvious notes of fruity apple combined with some caramel and oak. Reposado, or rested, tequila has spent time in used American whiskey barrels, so it's softened and has taken in oak flavors as well as developed sweeter citrus and vanilla notes. These two create a blend that challenges the palate. Try this served hot with lemon and apple cider in winter for a change-up to a standard mulled cocktail.

The real technique to discovering combinations that work for you lies in trusting your own flavor memory. If you're reading this book, you're probably at least 21 years old. That means you have 21 years of flavor memories catalogued in your mind. Spirits are no different—just start making tasting notes so that you can refer back to them when needed. Look for initial complementary flavors first. Then seek out secondary flavors that might not be so obvious and go from there.

Consider this too: You can picture flavors in your mind without having to try them;

theoretical combinations that you know will or won't work out. If you can honestly say to yourself that you love anchovies because they're salty and oily and fishy, that's great. If you can also say you have an equal amount of love for chocolate ice cream because it's creamy and chocolatey and smooth, that's equally great. But do you really need to try them together to know how that pairing might play out? Probably not. Trust your instincts and use your imagination.

The fascinating thing in this thought experiment is this: if you think those two flavors will work in concert with each other, then they will—for you. There are many universal combinations we all seem to love: chocolate and almonds, French fries and ketchup, peas and carrots, etc. But, within each individual are some outliers that only work for them. For example, I like peanut butter on my tuna sandwiches, an idea I got while enjoying a dish of seared tuna with Thai peanut sauce.

The point is, you bought the booze. There's no wrong way to drink it, save for incredibly irresponsibly, no matter what the distillers might say. At the end of the day, they made that bottle for you. Do with it what you will.

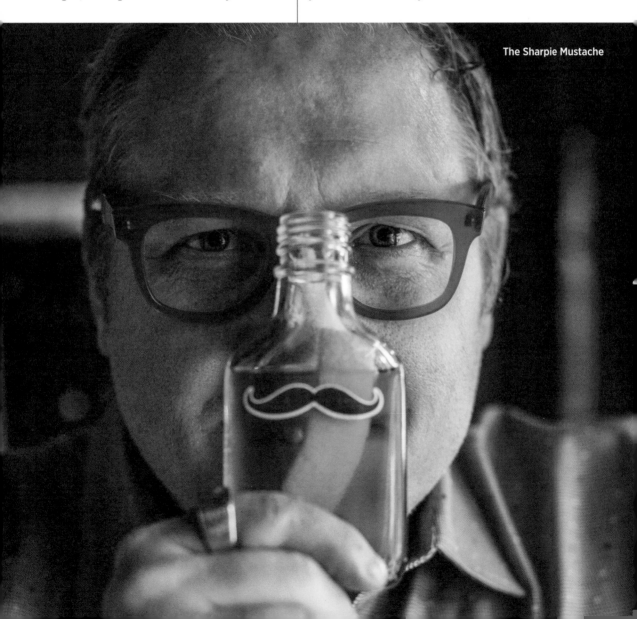

The Sharpie Mustache

Guatemalan Square
with the Vieux Carré

GUATEMALAN SQUARE

2 dashes Angostura bitters

2 dashes Peychaud's bitters

.25 oz Pierre Ferrand Dry Curaçao

.5 oz Carpano Antica

.5 oz Rittenhouse rye

1 oz Zacapa 23 Rum

Stir all ingredients in a mixing glass to chill and combine. Strain into a chilled Cocktail glass.

Garnish with an orange twist.

VIEUX CARRÉ

1 dash Angostura bitters

1 dash Peychaud's bitters

.5 tsp Bénédictine

.75 oz sweet vermouth

.75 oz rye

.75 oz Cognac

Stir all ingredients in a mixing glass to chill and combine. Serve on the rocks.

Garnish with an orange twist.

The Vieux Carré cocktail carries a noble pedigree. Hailing from cocktail ground zero New Orleans, it was created at the historic Hotel Monteleone in 1938 by head bartender Walter Bergeron. The name translates from French to mean "old square" and references what we more commonly know as the French Quarter. It's basically a split-based Manhattan with an herbal liqueur modifier and a split-bittering agent. Spicy rye shares the stage with heady Cognac, and the two are tempered by Italian sweet vermouth. But then Bénédictine sweeps in to bring a honeyed sweetness backed up with hints of lemon. Baking spices from Angostura bitters plus the subtle anise from Peychaud's season the brew into a pleasing and complex balance. It's a drink that satisfies on many levels. I decided to change it up anyway.

In my Guatemalan Square, I pull at the same threads and shuffle the ingredients ever so slightly. The outcome is an entirely different amalgam with a new personality. In place of the Cognac, I call for a Guatemalan rum that's rich and carries thick aromas of vanilla and island spices. Standing in for Bénédictine is Dry Curaçao, not as sweet as regular Curaçao but still packed with citrus flavors from laraha, a variety of orange similar to the Valencia, that's grown on the tiny island of Curaçao. The remaining cast of ingredients and the proportions remain the same as in the original concoction. Only now, the drink rings out with flavors of sophisticated cocoa, vanilla and orange that would be as welcome on the tiny island of Curaçao as it would the island of Manhattan.

Rough Seas

I'm often asked to create cocktails for events and parties and to add my particularly bitter slant to them. Tiki by the Sea is an annual event held on the Jersey shore in a small town called Wildwood. This educational and informational gathering is hosted by Avua Cachaça at a small, family-owned hotel and attended by cocktail professionals with a love of or interest in Tiki culture. When Jägermeister asked me to not only make a drink but also to present it at the event, I jumped at the chance. Grassy and funky cachaça combined with sharp ginger syrup and smooth nutty orgeat is a delicious start. The addition of Jägermeister, with its flavors of grapefruit peel, ginger and anise really toss the tempest. Bitter aromatics from Peychaud's serve not only as flavor but also step in as garnish as well when used to paint the pebble ice. It's as beautiful to look at as it is tasty to drink and though it's Rough Seas, it'll be smooth sailing.

.75 oz ginger syrup (pg 244)

.75 oz orgeat (pg 246)

.75 oz lemon juice

1 oz Jägermeister

1 oz cachaça

Heavy dashes of Peychaud's Bitters

Whip shake with a few pebbles. Pour over fresh pebble ice in a swizzle glass. Mound more ice on top like a snow cone and paint with Peychaud's.

If you're interested in emulating the firey presentation seen at left, fill the juicer-pressed rind of half a lime with rum, then ignite it with an extended lighter or long-tipped match. Dust with cinnamon for a crackling effect.

MAKE YOUR OWN PEBBLE ICE

A handful of drink recipes within (and without) this book call for pebble ice. There are numerous reasons for this, among them that it dilutes drinks much faster than larger cubes, which is the goal for a drink like the Mint Julep (pg 73) or the Rough Seas. So what do you do if you don't have a machine that manufactures the stuff? Grab a large zip-top bag, fill it with ice cubes, wrap the whole thing in a dish towel and start smacking it against a counter until the ice breaks up. The towel should keep the ice from tearing through the bag. Alternatively, you can use a wooden hammer and/or a sturdy (and new) coin bag like you might find at a bank or in an office supply store, as they're practically puncture proof. It's tough to make a lot of pebble ice up front, as to keep it from melting you'll need to store it in your freezer, where it will inevitably morph back into larger chunks of ice. Of course all you need to do then is repeat the cycle and break that stuff up. If that sounds like too much work, you can go with the crushed ice function on a fancy refrigerator, try a rough chop with a blender or purchase a consumer grade pebble ice maker so you'll never have to hammer a bag again.

Sharpie Mustache

I'm often asked by my guests about the blending of gin with whiskey, which seems obvious to me when you consider the elementary components each brings to the mix. Gin is inherently herbal, while rye whiskey has a distinct spiciness. No one questions it when a chef mixes herbs and spices—why act confused when your bartender does the same? Created by my dear friend and colleague Chris Elford during his time at Amor y Amargo, this drink has become a staple item on the menu there (as well as numerous cocktail lists across the country), and is a stirring example of how exceptional the gin/whiskey combo can be. Add in Meletti, a Kola Nut amaro, featuring notes of vanilla, leather and baking spice and soften the concoction with Bonal, a floral aperitif, then sew it all together with hints of ginger, nutmeg and mace from the bitters. The result is a cocktail full of familiar flavors presented in a new way. It's delicious served up, but at Amor y Amargo we prepare them in advance and serve them in a flask—we go through several buckets-full on any given night. You might as well go through as much, though you should heed the cocktail's name: They go down so easily you may find yourself waking up sporting a Sharpie Mustache of your own.

2 dashes Bittermens
'Elemakule Tiki Bitters

.75 oz Amaro Meletti

.75 oz Bonal Gentiane Quina

.75 oz London Dry gin
(we use Beefeater)

.75 oz 100° rye whiskey
(we use Rittenhouse)

Stir with plenty of ice to chill and dilute. Serve up or in a 100ml glass flask.

Garnish with an orange twist.

BUILDING IN ADVANCE: THE ART (AND ATTRACTIVENESS) OF THE BATCH COCKTAIL

Why would you prepare cocktails in advance? I don't know—why do anything now that you could do tomorrow, Mr/s. Procrastinator? Beyond the convenience, batch cocktails are perfect when you're planning for a dinner party or larger gathering. It can be fun to bartend your party, but it's also a drag to be chained to the bar while everyone else is enjoying the party you're hosting, which is why many best laid plans for a fancy cocktail party quickly devolve into guests dumping a bunch of booze into solo cups and topping it with Hi-C.

Building batch cocktails yields ease of service and consistency of quality drinks while lifting the burden of labor considerably. This method is best for cocktails that don't involve any perishables, including juice, dairy, eggs or herbs. But if you're serving all-spirit cocktails such as Martinis, Manhattans and Negronis, there's no reason not to do it. Start by scaling up the measurements by the target number of servings, then add water to achieve the dilution from melted ice you'd normally get by shaking (55% of volume) or stirring (45% of volume). Built drinks require no water. Pour into bottles and chill in either your refrigerator or freezer, breaking them out when you're ready to drink.

Stolen Goat

This drink features my new favorite Genever, brought to market in 2017 by my dear friend Philip Duff. A native of Skerries, a small seaside town in Ireland, Duff's Old Duff Genever features a goat on its label, a direct reference to the local story of St. Patrick's goat. Legend has it St. Patrick had a goat on his island just off the coast of Ireland to supply him with milk. One day, while visiting the mainland to convert locals to Catholicism, some inhabitants of nearby Skerries took his goat and had a feast—the goat was not a guest. Enraged, St. Patrick confronted them, and when they tried to lie about what they'd done, they could only bleat like goats until they told the truth. From then on, the residents of the town have been referred to as Skerries Goats.

This swizzle-style drink plays on the maltiness of Old Duff Genever by adding a rich, nutty and bolder-style brandy to the mix. Strega, a liquor made from saffron (the threads of the crocus flower, and one of the most expensive spices on earth) brings both florality and sweetness, and lemon juice brightens and balances the drink. The oils from the rosemary add an extra vegetal and savory layer. The result is a drink that's beautiful, complex and easy drinking with a decided kick. Cheers, kid!

Rosemary sprigs

.75 oz Old Duff Genever

.75 oz Strega

.75 oz Cardenal Mendoza Brandy

.75 oz lemon juice

1.5 tsp of cane syrup

Heavy dashes Peychaud's Bitters

Press rosemary into the bottom of a glass. Swizzle (or whip and dirty pour) the next 5 ingredients with pebble ice. Top with more pebble ice and paint with Peychaud's.

Garnish with rosemary.

Grandmother's Tea

1 dash Bittermens
Orange Cream Citrate

.5 oz Strega

.5 oz Amaro Del Capo Amaro

1 oz blanc vermouth

1 oz Louis Royer Force 53
Cognac

Stir first 5 ingredients over plenty
of ice to chill and dilute. Strain into
a Rocks glass over fresh ice. Easily
scaled up for a pitcher.

*Garnish with orange and lemon
twists.*

I had the good fortune of visiting Cognac and Jarnac France
with Nicolas Royer (sixth generation of the venerable Royer Cognac
house). While on our tour, he'd scheduled a day to visit his grandmère
at her chateau on one of their vineyards. As a good Southern boy, I have
a tremendous affection for my own grandmother and was excited at the
prospect of meeting his. We arrived early in the afternoon and were
greeted on her beautiful front porch overlooking the vineyard. She was
as gracious as I expected, offering us pastry and giving us a tour of the
grounds. It remains my fondest memory of the trip.

Upon arriving back at my bar, I set myself to the task of creating a
drink to solidify my memories of the entire experience in France. Nick's
grandmother immediately came to mind. I created this drink to remind
me of her, as well as my own grandmother, who would always greet
visitors on her front porch with iced tea. Combining the orange and herb
flavor from Del Capo with the florality of Strega and the fruity nature
of the Royer family's Cognac, this drink is meant to mimic the flavors of
Southern-style iced tea while packing the punch of 106-proof Cognac.
After all, it's Grandmother's Tea: Only for grown-ups.

GUEST BARTENDER **SARAH MORISSEY**

Deacon Blues

Sarah Morrissey is an NYC colleague of mine. A great bartender who knows how to deliver warm hospitality and backs up her charisma with a talent for making award-winning drinks, she responded immediately and enthusiastically when I reached out and asked her if she'd like to contribute to this book. The Deacon Blues is an Old Fashioned-style cocktail with a syrup made from fresh ground black pepper and Madagascar vanilla beans. Sarah is a fan of the band Steely Dan, and I imagine her listening to the song in the background ("...drink Scotch whisky all night long...") as she first concocted this drink. As it turns out, that's pretty much how she came up with the name.

"I entered an Old Fashioned competition, where we had to take the classic drink and put our spin on it," says Sarah. "I knew I wanted Angostura bitters and overproof bourbon but was perplexed at what else to use in the drink. I was listening to 'Deacon Blues' by Steely Dan, and I thought 'Shit, how is there not a drink named after this song?!' So I decided to use a small amount of scotch for a smokey note, and I accidentally put black pepper in my vanilla syrup and actually loved it."

Spicy and rich, the syrup lends it a sweet and savory quality. Further, the spirit is split between bold overproof bourbon whiskey and smoky mezcal which gives the whole drink a spectacular sweet and savory flavor profile. "Everything seemed great in my original version, but the scotch overpowered the bourbon, and I knew I wouldn't win the competition with a scotch-forward drink, so I switched to a more mellow, fruit-forward mezcal, and it worked beautifully," adds Sarah. "The two different spirits really blend well together, and the spicy-sweet syrup marries the flavors."

Though Sarah prefers to create this cocktail one drink at a time, if you're throwing a party, consider preparing a bunch in advance, as these are going to please the crowd. "You want to make sure to stir it over ice so it's cold. You can always cut lime twists ahead of time, and a nice crack of fresh black pepper on top really sends it over the edge," says Sarah. "It may not have that much to do with 'Deacon Blues' anymore, but it tastes great!"

4 dashes Angostura bitters

.25 oz black pepper vanilla syrup (pg 245)

.5 oz Agave de Cortes mezcal

1.5 oz Old Forester 100-proof bourbon

Build in glass, add ice, stir.

Garnish with a lime twist and 2 cracks of black pepper.

Hanky Panky

Essentially a sweet gin martini bolstered with a few dashes of the bitter and herbal elixir Fernet-Branca, the Hanky Panky's aroma is further enhanced by orange oil from a fresh twist. Ada Coleman created this classic cocktail during her 23-year stint from 1903–1926 as the first female head bartender at The American Bar at the Savoy Hotel in London, widely considered to be one of the best bars in the world. A female bartender was a rarity at the time, never mind head bartender at a spot with international acclaim. Known affectionately as Coley, Ada was host to a clientele of expats, everyday Londoners and the stars of the time (Marlene Dietrich, Charlie Chaplin and Mark Twain were among her regular customers). She'd engage them in lively conversation as well as serve the popular drinks of the day, and it's reported she'd often extend the party and her own hospitality by having them over to her house for cocktails, singing and dancing well into the evening.

Arguably the world's most famous female bartender to date, when she retired, five papers deemed the story newsworthy. "'Coley' is known to thousands of people all over the world, Britons who are now roughing it in various parts of the Empire, Americans who think of her every time they remember their own country's dryness," *The Daily Express* reported when her retirement was announced in December of 1925.

It's notable that at the time in the common vernacular of England that "hanky panky" didn't mean what we take it to mean today. Much more innocently, it simply meant "magic." For me, the most magical thing about this drink is just how well it holds up, given that it was created nearly a century before the "cocktail revolution" began.

Classic **COCKTAIL**

1.5 oz sweet vermouth

1.5 oz gin

2 dashes Fernet-Branca

Stir ingredients well in a mixing glass to chill and dilute, then strain into a chilled Nick & Nora glass.

Orange twist, discarded.

A QUICK LOOK AT HERBALS

This informal category with wide-ranging variety started with a devotion to God.

In categorizing my backbar, I differentiate between what I deem "herbals" and amari. Though the definition may be very similar (amaro being "an Italian bittersweet herbal liquor"), there's a fundamental difference between the two. Herbals often contain some bittering components, but due to their much higher sugar content, they aren't bitter enough to be lumped in with amaro, nor are amari (all containing a sweetener) sweet enough to be considered herbals. It's a fundamental shift in ratio; more of one component with less of another creates an entirely new product. To throw things back to the kitchen, as I often do, mayonnaise is mayonnaise is mayonnaise until you add a bit of garlic to it. Suddenly it's no longer mayonnaise—it's aioli. In the case of herbals, the sweetness is the catalyst, the driving factor behind why they deserve their own categorization. For example, if a heaping dose of quinine found its way into Chartreuse, and half the sweetener was removed, it'd probably be an amazing amaro. But as it stands, it's so sweet you can barely tell it's also bitter. And because "amaro" means bitter, sweet herbal liqueurs don't really fit the name.

The production of herbals was started, in large part, by monks. Monasticism, from the Latin "monachos" meaning "solitary person," offers spiritual purpose and hope for salvation for (mostly) men who lived quiet, meditative lives of service. It may seem ironic then that these early monks also created some of the most delicious (and potent!) booze in the known world. Due to their de facto isolation, monasteries needed to be somewhat self sufficient in their operations, with gardens and livestock yielding goods to harvest and eat. During the middle ages, monks also ran the hospitals of the era, helping the sick as best they could and providing shelter and food for travelers; a "hospitaller" was in charge of looking after visitors and is likely where we derive the word hospitality from.

Given the free flow of information we live with today, we might easily overlook the fact that very few people were educated enough to read during these times. Monks were far ahead of the curve in this regard. The fact that they could read and write meant they could produce and, more importantly, reproduce products from a recipe. Many of those recipes were for elixirs the monks would create by foraging herbs, barks, roots and flowers they'd then macerate with wine or distillates to make remedies for the ails of those under their care. These early recipes were closely guarded secrets then and remain so today, even though their medicinal aspect has faded away. The elixirs were also used to barter for any goods the monks couldn't create on their own, which

explains how each monastery's signature blend started to gain notoriety.

Today, due to a newfound interest in the category, distillers of all manner and location are revisiting these types of liqueurs as well as creating new ones to add to their portfolios (they're already producing a distillate, and adding a macerate to their base is an easy way to get more money out of it). But I still prefer the classics. After all, if something's been practically perfect for 400 years, why mess with it?

There are a few bottles on my backbar that are herbal, yet do not fit the profile to be categorized as amaro as they're too high in brix (sugar content) making them far too sweet for that designation. Most of these were created for medicinal purposes and include things like Sapins, which tastes distinctly of fir trees, Génépy, an alpine liqueur, Absinthe and, of course, Chartreuse with its 130+ botanicals. I use these to add both a layer of sweetness as well as a bright pop of herbal aroma and flavor.

Common Examples of Herbals include...

Chartreuse
Made by Carthusian monks in France since 1737 from a 1605 recipe using a blend of 130+ botanicals. Green Chartreuse clocks in at a whopping 110 proof. Yellow Chartreuse, a bit milder and also more sweet, is 80 proof.

Bénédictine
Not created by the namesake monks, rather by Alexandre Le Grand in the 19th century, Bénédictine boasts 27 herbs and spices. Its label bears the initials D. O. M., which stands for "Deo Optimo Maximo" (To God, most good, most great).

Génépy
Mostly derived from Artemisia plants (aka wormwood), Génépy is produced in the alpine regions of Europe.

Kümmel
First produced in 16th century Netherlands, flavored with cumin, caraway and fennel seeds.

Absinthe
High in ABV and heavily flavored with fennel, anise and grand wormwood. Though not typically sweetened, absinthe's natural sweetness makes it an outlier but still a member of this category.

Pastis
Herbal liqueur with the addition of star anise distillate, differentiating it from absinthe's European green anise.

Herbsaint
Originally produced in 1934 as an absinthe substitute in New Orleans, Herbsaint contains high amounts of licorice and anise flavors.

Drambuie
Scotch-based honey and herb liquor. The name comes from Scottish Gaelic and means "the drink that satisfies." Combine 1 part with 2 parts scotch for the classic Rusty Nail.

GUEST BARTENDER **NICK BENNETT**

Aged Eggnog

Nick Bennett and I have manned three bars as well as traveled to Italy together. He's more than just a colleague—he's a trusted friend. We also drank in the interests of science while working at Booker & Dax, a bar founded on the principles of molecular gastronomy. We had all manner of gadgets and tools at our disposal: rotovaps, immersion circulators, vacuum sealers, red-hot pokers and more! We used them to make impossible drinks impossibly delicious.

Now he's the head barman at Porchlight in NYC where he mixes no less interesting or delicious drinks, though they are often far less complicated. Among the things he learned during his studies is how alcohol by volume affects perishables like cream and eggs. Thus, his Aged Eggnog came to be. I'm a fan of eggnog as an occasion-based drink. Nick, on the other hand, is a man obsessed. "If I could drink it all year long I would, though I am pretty sure it wouldn't be as enjoyable on a hot, summer day," says Nick.

For this recipe, a touch of Jamaican rum adds a slight funky quality to bridge the bourbon and brandy together, and the heavy cream is just enough to add a little more body without making it feel too thick. "As for the spices, if you want to add more and make it a Christmas medley of spices you are welcome to, but I'm generally happy with just a few grates of fresh nutmeg," adds Nick.

Whip this up once the holiday season rolls around, or—if you're feeling adventurous—give aging it a try. "The first few times I aged it I just put it in an airtight, sanitized container and threw it in my cupboard and forgot about it for a year." Both Nick and I would like to stress that if you are going to experiment with this approach, sanitizing the container you're going to use is the most important step. From there, it's a waiting game. "Every week or so when I remember to, I shake it up a little bit. I don't want anything settling on the bottom or anything with different densities resting on top of another," says Nick. "And the reason I leave it in the cupboard is for a consistent temperature. I was worried more about fluctuating temperatures than it being at almost room temperature. I've never had any problems with it." You can take Nick's lead and age yours in a dark cabinet or, as I do, in the refrigerator. From there it's all about presentation and salesmanship. "I drink gallons of the stuff, but all of my friends that I would give samples to were more hesitant to try the cupboard version than the ones I started keeping in the refrigerator," says Nick. "I think it's a mental thing." Aging eggnog is certainly mental—but in this case, it's just crazy enough to work.

.25 oz heavy cream

.5 oz demerara syrup

.75 oz whole milk

Whole egg

.5 oz Laird's Apple Brandy

.5 oz Jamaican rum

1 oz Wild Turkey Bourbon 101

Build in a mixer with ice. Whip shake and strain. Serve in a wine glass (or store in an airtight glass container for up to a year)

Garnish with freshly grated nutmeg.

Smoke & Mirrors

2 dashes orange bitters

.5 oz Noilly Pratt dry vermouth

.5 oz Amontillado sherry

.5 oz Laphroaig 10-Year

1.5 oz NY Distillery Dorothy Parker Gin

Stir all ingredients with plenty of ice. Strain into a chilled Cocktail glass.

Garnish with a flamed orange twist.

Another example of mixed base cocktail design, this drink is basically an augmented gin martini featuring New York Distilling Company's Dorothy Parker gin. Proprietor Allen Katz named his American gin after the firebrand writer and critic best known for her sharp observations and quick wit (she famously said "I like to have a martini, two at the very most. After three I'm under the table, after four I'm under my host...."). Her namesake gin features a lineup of usual suspects on the gin botanicals list with the notable inclusion of elderberries and cinnamon.

As for the rest of the drink, hints of wood and toasted nuts are present from the sherry with a soft roundness from the dry vermouth. Finally, the peated scotch stands up and offers a warm smoky greeting in a concoction that's nearly as clear as water—a true magic act. Dare I say it'll be easy for you to make disappear? I do dare say that.

How Do I Compare

This is a Scaffa, or room temperature cocktail. Bold notes of apple are pushed forward by the bourbon and the bitters, while orange notes abound with the Cointreau and orange twist. How do I compare apples to oranges? I don't. I just drink them.

2 dashes apple bitters

.25 oz Cointreau

.5 oz Bénédictine

.75 oz bourbon

.75 oz apple brandy

Pour all ingredients into a Rocks glass without ice.

Orange twist, discarded.

Island Time

If I were to describe this cocktail as an experience rather than a series of flavors, I'd say it's a lot like drinking a daiquiri while enjoying a cigar, which is to say it's got some tastes of the tropics that are enhanced by and in harmony with the smoky notes from the Chinese rhubarb in the Zucca. They all benefit from the playful funk of Agricole Rhum in this frappe, a relaxing tipple that's worth your time, particularly on a day when time is the last thing on your mind.

1 dash Scrappy's Lime Bitters

1 oz lime juice

.75 oz Zucca Rabarbo

2 oz Rhum Agricole

Whip shake all ingredients with a few pebbles of ice until they melt away. Pour into a double Old Fashioned filled with pebble ice.

No garnish.

Brawny Man

Not for the faint of heart, this is a massive attack on the palate. Dell'Erborista is an unfiltered gentian and honey amaro that tastes of the forest floor in spring. Punt y Mes toes the line between vermouth and amaro. Gran Classico tastes of burnt orange and caramel. All of this combines with big hits of smoke from the scotch. It comes at you as bitter, bitter, smoky and bitter. The scant amount of coffee amaro from Kansas City's J. Rieger & Co. completes this masterpiece of masculinity. Note: women can drink it too.

.25 oz J. Rieger Caffé Amaro

.75 oz peated scotch

.75 oz Punt y Mes

.75 oz Gran Classico

.75 oz Varnelli Amaro Dell'Erborista

Stir all ingredients to chill with ice and dilute. Strain into a chilled Rocks glass without ice.

Garnish with orange twist.

Black Tie Affair

Fresh rosemary sprig

.5 oz lime juice

.75 oz pineapple juice

.5 oz green Chartreuse

1 oz Black Strap Cruzan rum

1 oz rye whiskey

Press rosemary into bottom of a Collins glass. Whip shake remaining ingredients with a few pebbles of ice and dirty pour over fresh pebble ice in a Collins glass. Top with even more pebble ice.

Garnish with rosemary.

Founded in 1760, the Cruzan distillery on the island of St. Croix carries the claim of "the most honored rum distillery in the world." Though they produce a lengthy portfolio of rums, it's Black Strap that has the attention of craft bartenders around the globe, and I'm certainly guilty of furthering the trend. This cocktail was the result of a little experimentation with it, and the results are worth dressing up for.

I adore the combination of pineapple and anise in tropically inspired cocktails, and this drink has it in spades. The Black Strap rum has thick, funky aromas of molasses and hints of licorice, both of which are fortified by the herbal nature of Chartreuse. Pressing the rosemary into the bottom of the glass expresses its oils to release more herbal fragrance, and the rye steps in to calm the sweetness with its assertive, spicy backbone. Not to be taken lightly, this is only a poolside drink if the party starts at 10 p.m.

HOW TO MAKE A TOAST

If you're at a black tie affair as opposed to merely drinking one, there's a pretty good chance you'll be involved in a toast of some sort. If you're the person making it, there are a few things to bear in mind. Toasting is born out of the tradition of making a wish or saying a prayer to god(s), which is why we raise our glasses as opposed to keeping them in front of our chests. Because the toast is an offering, it's considered bad luck (and form) to toast with an empty glass. But toasting with water is even worse. To offer the gods water could be an insult and result in them treating you less than favorably. In fact, the Greeks believed the dead traveled to the underworld via the river Lethe and would drink from it along the way to erase the memories of their life. Raising a glass of water during a toast could be construed as wishing death upon the guest of honor, or even oneself. Finally, the toast is effectively starting a new phase of the party, which means brevity is the watchword. A long, droning toast does very little to encourage anticipation. Keep things simple and civil, don't force a joke and when you touch glasses be sure to look your fellow toaster in the eyes. It's good luck, or at least good form.

Upper Crust

.5 oz orgeat

.75 oz lemon juice

.25 oz Maraschino liqueur

.5 oz Old Tom gin

1 oz Cognac

Shake and strain into a sugar rimmed Nic and Nora glass.

Garnish with a long, wide lemon twist.

The more I think about it, the more I notice how much gin I slip into drinks. In this instance, Old Tom takes the stage to add herbal sweetness to a Cognac cocktail with a somewhat tropical vibe. However, the real secret ingredient to this cocktail is the addition of Maraschino liqueur. The distillate of Marasca cherries and pits, it's simultaneously sweet and dry, and it helps amplify the fruity and slightly cocoa qualities from the Cognac. Luxardo is the most popular, but there are others and I encourage you to try a few and find one(s) that you prefer.

ORGEAT

This is a compound syrup typically made from almonds, sugar and rose or orange flower water. Previously it was made from a combination of ground barley and derives its name from the Latin through French word *orge* meaning barley. Several commercial varieties, including some that use other nuts such as macadamia and walnut, are available. You can order many online, but they tend to be too sweet for my taste. I'm partial to Orgeat Works by Tiki Adam or Beachbum Berry's Latitude 29. However, given how easy orgeat is to make, I'd recommend putting in the effort to create it yourself. It's a handy product to have if you're making tiki or tropical drinks. Plus, it'll liven up your morning coffee or even your pancakes. You'll find my recipe on page 246.

Shipwrecked

.5 oz amber agave nectar

.75 oz lime juice

.5 oz Del Maguey Vida Mezcal

1.5 oz El Dorado 8-Year Rum

Shake with ice and strain into a chilled Coupe glass.

Garnish with a lime wheel.

It's my experience that overcomplicating drinks with too many ingredients leads to cocktails that have few defining characteristics and are less than the sum of their parts. As such, I like to keep things simple when I can, recognizing that simple and simplistic are not the same. This drink follows a very common, straightforward format (that of the Daiquiri [pg 174]), but the swap of one quarter of the rum for mezcal and the total substitution of agave nectar for simple syrup results in a completely new, far more complex flavor experience. Dark rum, when augmented with mezcal, becomes a smoky sweet juggernaut slightly tamed by the lime juice. Agave has a richer texture that coats the tongue and helps the flavors adhere. But be forewarned: This drink, in the wrong hands, could wreck you.

GUEST BARTENDER **franky marshall**

Guillotine

.25 oz honey syrup (pg 244)

.25 oz Giffard
Crème de Banane Liqueur

.75 oz blended scotch whisky

1 oz mezcal

Stir all ingredients with plenty of ice in a large mixing glass. Strain into a Strain into a Snifter over a large-format ice cube.

Lemon twist, discarded.

franky marshall, who for reasons that are her own asked that I not capitalize her name, is among the most intelligent bartenders I've ever encountered. She's thoughtful in her combinations and driven in her methods, all while being gracious and hospitable. She carries herself with a unique aura, announcing her presence in a room without having to say a word. A world traveler constantly seeking more knowledge about spirits and cocktails, she oversees operations at Le Boudoir, a Brooklyn-based bar outfitted like Marie Antoinette's favorite sitting room. It seems to embody marshall's style in every way—as does her cocktail, Guillotine.

Reaching first to Mexico then to far away Scotland and finally to France, this cocktail is also a world traveler. When I taste it I'm transported to all those places at once. Blended scotch has inherent notes of banana and, though it doesn't have the rich smoke of a peated scotch, the mezcal comes in to drive that note forward.

"The two base spirits—mezcal and scotch—can have varying degrees of smokiness depending on the style, so the intensity level can be adjusted to suit your mood or your guest's palate," says franky. "I first made it as a spontaneous creation for a guest who wanted a shaken 'scotchtail.' It originally had mint and lemon juice but no banana liqueur. Then when I was working on drinks for the first menu at Le Boudoir, I decided to revisit it, but as a stirred sipper."

All the aromas inherent in the drink are captured in the brandy snifter and burst into the nose at every sip. And if you think it only smells good..."A guest once referred to this cocktail as 'The most pleasant of kicks in the face,'" laughs franky. "I think that sums it up nicely." I concur.

2 dashes Angostura bitters

.5 oz pineapple shrub

.5 oz lime juice

1 oz London Dry gin

1 oz Pierre Ferrand 1840 Cognac

Ginger beer

Combine first five ingredients in a Highball glass. Add ice and gently stir. Pour ginger beer down the spiral of a bar spoon to fill.

Garnish with candied ginger.

Suffering Fools

I was recently asked what cocktail I'd be if I were one. I tried to be thoughtful in my response and chose the Suffering Bastard, a classic created in 1942 in Cairo to help British officers overcome their hangovers, with a name that fits my occasionally gruff personality. However, if I had been given more time, I'd likely have said this riff on the classic was more my style. In this version, bourbon is replaced by Cognac, giving the drink a more floral aroma. The lime juice is split with fresh pineapple shrub creating a more tropically inspired tipple with an interesting acidic slant. I use a spicy ginger beer like Reed's to top it off, and they make a great candied ginger to complete the picture.

Now I See

St Raphaël is rich with vanilla, cocoa, orange peel and gentian—oxidized grapes give it a sherry like flavor. Tosolini tastes of cinnamon, root beer and rhubarb. Aged for four months in ash barrels, it's soft on the palate. When combined with brandy, these elements create jammy notes of dried fruit and oxidized raisins with hints of baking spice and toffee, to create a cocktail tailor made for sipping in a big leather chair surrounded by rich mahogany and leather bound books. Or watching *Anchorman*.

2 dashes AZ Bitters Lab Figgy Pudding bitters

.5 oz Amaro Tosolini

.1 oz St. Raphaël

1.5 oz brandy

Stir with plenty of ice. Strain into a double Old Fashioned glass over a large chunk of ice.

Garnish with an orange twist.

Zipper Skin

Zipper Skins are a variety of Dancy tangerine whose skins are easily peeled or zipped off. This drink is plentiful with orange flavors: China China is an orange and herb amaro that has notes of charred orange marmalade. Southern Amaro is made by High Wire Distilling in Charleston, SC. Made from gentian, mint, black tea and Dancy tangerines, it's rich and flavorful and brings this whole concoction together in Southern style. Though it's a sipper, it zips down fast.

2 dashes Cocktailpunk Smoked Orange Bitters

1 oz bourbon

1 oz Bigallet China China

1 oz High Wire Distilling Southern Amaro

Build in a Old Fashioned glass. Add ice and gently stir to combine.

Orange twist, discarded.

Disco Ball

Based on a shot of the same name (equal parts mezcal, green and yellow Chartreuse), I added a little dry vermouth and altered the equal parts original to be a longer and more sophisticated cocktail that is simultaneously sweet and smokey. It'll have you putting on your boogie shoes, while still leaving you in prime dancing shape.

2 dashes Devil's Larder Chamomile bitters

.5 oz green Chartreuse

.5 oz yellow Chartreuse

1 oz blanc vermouth

1 oz mezcal

Stir first five ingredients in a mixing glass with plenty of ice to chill and dilute. Strain into a chilled Cocktail glass.

Lemon twist, discarded.

APPENDIX
The fine print on some fine recipes.

SYRUPS

BASIC SIMPLE SYRUP

1 cup sugar

1 cup water

Combine sugar and water over heat. Bring to a simmer and stir to dissolve sugar. Allow to cool to room temperature. Store in the fridge.

FOR GINGER SYRUP, use Basic Simple Syrup recipe, but sub out water for ginger juice.

FOR HIBISCUS (OR ANY) TEA SYRUP, use Basic Simple Syrup recipe, but sub out water for triple strength tea. This also works with coffee.

HEAVY SIMPLE SYRUP

2 cups sugar

1 cup water

Combine sugar and water over heat. Bring to a simmer and stir to dissolve sugar. Allow to cool to room temperature. Store in the fridge.

HONEY SIMPLE SYRUP

1 cup honey

1 cup water

Heat water to a simmer. Add honey and stir to dissolve. Allow to cool to room temperature. Store in the fridge.

BROWN SIMPLE SYRUP

2 cups dark brown sugar

1 cup water

Combine sugar and water over heat. Bring to a simmer and stir to dissolve sugar. Allow to cool to room temperature. Store in the fridge.

PRETTY MUCH ANY FRUIT OR BERRY SYRUP
Including raspberry, passion fruit, tart cherry, blackberry and more...

2 cups demerara sugar

1 cup water

1 cup fruit (fresh or frozen)

Stir sugar and water over low heat until sugar has dissolved. Add fruit stirring until it forms a pulp. Strain to remove seeds and bits and pour into a jar and refrigerate. Over time, the pectin will rise to the surface and can be skimmed off.

RHUBARB SYRUP

2 cups demerara sugar

1 cup water

1 cup chopped rhubarb

Stir sugar and water over low heat until sugar has dissolved. Add rhubarb, stirring until it softens. Strain to remove rhubarb, pour into a jar and refrigerate.

CINNAMON AND CLOVE INFUSED SIMPLE SYRUP

1 cup sugar

1 cup water

5 sticks cinnamon

1 tsp whole cloves

Combine sugar and water over heat. Bring to a simmer and add cinnamon sticks and cloves. Stir to dissolve sugar. Cover and allow to cool to room temperature. Strain and store in the fridge.

NOTE This recipe can serve as a template for any "infused" syrup. Want to make an allspice syrup? Throw some allspice berries into the simmering water and make magic. Want a spicy syrup? Try adding dried ancho chilies. Just make sure you cover the syrup as it cools to enhance the infusion process.

BLACK PEPPER SYRUP

1 cup simple syrup

1 vanilla pod, split open

50 cracks of black pepper

Scrape inside of vanilla pod to add seeds to syrup. Top with 50 cracks of black pepper from a pepper grinder. Stir gently to mix. Do not strain. Let sit refrigerated overnight before using.

BURNT SUGAR SYRUP

1 cup granulated white sugar

.75 cup very hot water

Place sugar in a medium saucepan over high heat. Stirring constantly, cook until the sugar melts, about 5 minutes. The sugar will try to seize during the process, so keep stirring. Cook until dark brown and foamy with whips of smoke, then remove from heat. Stirring constantly, pour in the hot water. It will splatter a lot, so be careful. Once fully incorporated, return to medium-high heat and cook until the syrup thickens slightly. Cool completely before use.

FALERNUM
This flavored syrup can be simply flavored or far more complex. Try

adding cinnamon, peppercorns, honey—whatever you like.

2 oz slivered almonds

1 Tbsp whole cloves

Fine zest of 4 large limes (reserve the juice)

Fine zest of 2 large grapefruits (drink the juice?)

Fine diced ginger from a 2" piece

Several drops almond extract

2 cups sugar

2 cups water

4 oz overproof rum (I prefer Wray & Nephew)

Toast the almonds and cloves in a pan over medium heat until fragrant and reserve in a large glass jar with zest and ginger. Pour in the rum and allow to steep for 24 hours. The following day, over low heat, dissolve the sugar in the water. Remove from heat and allow to cool to room temperature. Strain the solids from the rum and discard them. Add the syrup and the lime juice to the rum. Add a few drops of almond extract and taste. Add more if you like. Store refrigerated for up to six weeks.

SHRUBS

Shrubs are essentially syrups where the water has been replaced with vinegar. As such, any of my syrups could be turned into shrubs if you sub in vinegar for the water.

If you're using fruit that has a lot of seeds, I recommend straining the shrub before using it in any drinks. If you're using ingredients that are seed free, you can opt to puree the entire mixture for a denser, more flavorful concoction.

PINEAPPLE GINGER SHRUB

1 cup apple cider vinegar

1 cup sugar

.75 cup pineapple, small dice

.75 cup fresh ginger, minced

Gently simmer all ingredients for 10-15 minutes. Allow to cool and strain or puree. Store in the fridge.

RASPBERRY (OR OTHER FRUIT) SHRUB

1 cup apple cider vinegar

1 cup sugar

1.5 cups fruit (fresh or frozen)

Gently simmer all ingredients for 10-15 minutes. Allow to cool and strain. Store in the fridge.

NOTE The above format can serve as a template for any flavors that strike your fancy. That goes for the vinegar as well. You can use balsamic vinegar in a fig-based shrub, or white vinegar in a cucumber-basil compound shrub. The sky's the limit.

HOUSEMADE GRENADINE

2 cups pomegranate juice

2 cups sugar

4 medium sized oranges

1-2 tsp orange flower water

Over medium heat, reduce the juice by half to 1 cup. Meanwhile, peel the oranges down to the white pith. (Use the fruit for juicing, no waste!) Stir in the sugar to dissolve. Add orange peels and remove from heat. Cover and allow to cool. Stir in orange flower water to taste. Strain and refrigerate. Will last three weeks refrigerated. Shelf life can be extended by adding 1 oz of an overproof spirit such as vodka.

HOMEMADE SARSAPARILLA

.75 cup water

.33 cup sugar

.75 tsp Zatarain's Root Beer extract

16 oz seltzer

Over low heat, dissolve the sugar into the water. Cool to room temperature and add the root beer concentrate, then chill. If using to make the Ranch Hand (pg 89), wait to add the seltzer until you're ready to bottle the drink to keep the soda from going flat prematurely. Otherwise, add the seltzer whenever you're ready for a refreshing glass of homemade root beer.

RAINBOW ROOM BERRY MARINADE

Pint of strawberries

Pint of blueberries

Pint of raspberries

2 oz VS Cognac

2 oz Cointreau

2 Tbsp sugar

Hull and quarter the strawberries, then mix them with the other berries in a bowl. Stir in the spirits and the sugar and set aside, stirring occasionally. The mix needs a couple hours to work; the sugar will work on the berries to pull out juice. Use as a garnish on Dale DeGroff's Blackberry Julep (pg 39), your own version of Baked Alaska or over ice cream.

OLEO SACCHRUM

A key ingredient in many classic punch

recipes, Oleo Sacchrum, which literally translates to oil-sugar, is easy to make and will level up your bartending credibility. You can make it with any citrus fruit.

1-2 whole peels from citrus fruit

1 cup superfine sugar

1 plastic zip top bag

Peel your citrus of choice, avoiding as much of the white pith as you can. Put the twists in a zip top bag and bury in superfine sugar. Squeeze out all the air (better, dip the bag in a sink of water and zip it closed before it's submerged or better still, use a vacuum sealer). Leave in sugar overnight, then pour off into a bottle, straining out the spent peels. Store for up to three weeks.

RYE CORDIAL

1 liter rye

1.5 cups whole espresso beans

Orange peels from 6 large oranges (as little white pith as possible)

1.5 cups dark brown sugar

Combine all ingredients in a large glass jar. Shake to dissolve sugar. Allow to sit for at least a week prior to tasting. Once the desired flavor is achieved, strain out and discard the solids. Pour back into a bottle and store on a shelf for use at any time.

ORGEAT
The tasty secret ingredients that makes many tiki tipples tick, orgeat is as easy to make as it is delicious to consume.

2 cups raw almonds (or any other nut. Literally, go nuts!)

1.5 cups sugar

1.5 cups water

.5 oz orange flower water

.5 oz Wray & Nephew rum*

In a 400°F oven, toast the nuts until fragrant. (You can vary the level of toast to achieve different layers of flavor, or use raw nuts for a slightly sweeter outcome.) Allow the nuts to cool to room temperature. Pulse in a food processor until coarsely ground. Add to a saucepan with the sugar and water. Bring to a simmer and cook, stirring for 5 minutes. Remove from heat, cover and allow to cool to room temperature. Strain through several layers of cheesecloth and add in the orange flower water and spirit. Store refrigerated for up to three weeks.

*__NOTE__ You can also use overproof vodka or really any spirit you'd like to marry with the flavor you're targeting. I choose rum as I typically use orgeat in tiki style drinks and it works for me.

BOURBON HOT COCOA
COCOA MIX

2 cups powdered sugar

1 cup cocoa (Dutch-process preferred)

2.5 cups powdered milk

1 tsp salt

2 tsp cornstarch

.25 tsp cayenne pepper, or more to taste

Combine all ingredients. Add 5 oz of warm milk (or 3 oz milk, 2 oz bourbon) to 2 Tbsp of mix for hot cocoa.

GREEN CHARTREUSE MARSHMALLOWS
adapted from *Gourmet*, December 1998

1 cup confectioners' sugar

3.5 envelopes (2 Tbsp plus 2.5 tsp) unflavored gelatin

.5 cup cold water

2 cups granulated sugar

.5 cup agave syrup

.5 cup plus 3 Tbsp green Chartreuse

.25 tsp salt

2 large egg whites

.5 tsp vanilla

Oil the bottom and the sides of a 13- by 9- by 2-inch baking pan and dust the bottom and the sides with confectioners' sugar.

Beat the egg whites to stiff peaks and then set aside. In the bowl of a standing electric mixer or in a large bowl, sprinkle gelatin over cold water and let stand to soften.

In a heavy saucepan, cook the sugar, agave, .5 cup Chartreuse and salt over low heat, stirring with a wooden spoon, until sugar is dissolved. Increase the heat to medium to boil mixture, without stirring, until a candy or digital thermometer registers 240°F (about 12 minutes). Remove pan from heat and pour sugar mixture over gelatin mixture, stirring until gelatin is dissolved.

With a standing or a hand-held electric mixer, beat mixture on high speed until white, thick and nearly tripled in volume, about 6 minutes if using standing mixer or about 10 minutes if using hand-held mixer. Beat egg whites, vanilla and remaining 3 Tbsp Chartreuse into sugar mixture until just combined. Pour mixture into baking pan and sift .25 cup confectioners' sugar evenly over top. Let sit, uncovered, until firm, at least 3 hours, or up to one day.

Run a thin knife around edges of pan and invert pan onto a large cutting board. Lifting up one corner of inverted pan, with fingers loosen marshmallow and let drop onto cutting board. With a large knife trim edges of marshmallow and cut marshmallow into 1.5-inch squares. Sift remaining confectioners' sugar into a large bowl and add marshmallows in batches, tossing to evenly coat.

CHAI-INFUSED COGNAC

16 oz Cognac

4 Chai tea bags

Let tea bags steep in Cognac for 2–3 hours. Strain and store in a sealable jar in the fridge for up to one week.

SALT PEANUTS WHISKEY

ROASTED PEANUT SYRUP

2 cups sugar

1 cup water

1 cup roasted peanuts

Over low heat, dissolve the sugar into the water. Add peanuts and stir. Remove from heat and cover. Let cool to room temperature. Strain through a fine mesh strainer. Discard the peanuts.

PEANUT-INFUSED BITTERS

.5 cup roasted peanuts, still warm from roasting

12-oz bottle Regan's Orange Bitters

Combine the two in a bowl and cover with plastic wrap. Allow to rest for 24 hours. Strain through a fine mesh or cheesecloth and return the liquid to the bitters bottle. Label it!

SALT SOLUTION

8 oz water

2 oz by weight kosher salt

Combine and shake to dissolve.

SOTHER'S HOT SAUCE
You can make yours however you like, but I like mine.

1 lb fresh chilies
(I like bird's eye), stemmed

2 Tbsp kosher salt

2 cups apple cider vinegar

2 cups fresh carrot juice

Put chilies and salt in a food processor and pulse to a coarse purée. Move purée to a 1-qt glass jar, loosely screw on lid, and let stand at room temperature for 24 hours to ferment slightly.

Stir in vinegar to cover and loosely screw on lid. Let sit at room temperature for at least one week.

Purée mixture in a blender on high until smooth. Strain through a fine mesh strainer sieve into a bowl. Add carrot juice to adjust flavor. The sauce may separate, shake vigorously before use.

SPICY-SWEET SALT

1 Tbsp refined sugar

5 Tbsp cayenne pepper

1 Tbsp kosher salt

Combine and keep handy in a small sealable container for rimming glasses for spicy Margaritas.

MANHATTAN GLAZED RIBS

RIBS

1 rack ribs

2 cups sweet vermouth reduced by half to 1 cup

1 cup Wild Turkey 101 Rye whiskey

.5 cup dark brown sugar

.25 cup ketchup

2 oz Worcestershire sauce

1 Tbsp Coleman's mustard powder

1 Tbsp onion powder

2 Tbsp smoked paprika

.5 oz Angostura bitters

In a small saucepan, combine all ingredients except bitters and ribs. Bring to a boil and cook over low until it reaches a glaze consistency. Remove from heat and stir in the bitters.

Cook ribs in your preferred method (I prefer to smoke mine, but they're your ribs). Halfway through cooking, brush with glaze. Repeat periodically until ribs are cooked.

MARTINI PICKLES

1 English cucumber sliced thin in a mandolin

1 Tbsp pickling spice (store-bought is fine)

1 small jalapeño split in half lengthwise

2 Tbsp sugar

4 oz apple cider vinegar

4 oz dry vermouth

4 oz London Dry gin

Bring the liquids and sugar to a simmer to dissolve. Place the cucumber and pepper in a small metal pot and place the pot in a bath of ice and water. Pour hot liquid over the cucumbers. Once cool, refrigerate for an additional 2 hours. Eat 'em.

INDEX

Consider this a shopping list.

ACKNOWLEDGEMENTS
The people to whom we all owe a drink

SOTHER TEAGUE

To Jeff Ashworth, my editor, for helping me shape my thoughts into words and those words into the paragraphs of this book. Additionally, I thank him for being a longtime friend and a damn fine bartender in his own right. To Eric Medsker, for capturing in photographs the feelings I have when a cocktail is presented to me. He's also a charismatic fellow and enthusiastic lover of cocktails himself, and it shows in each image (he further displays his talents by somehow making me look presentable). To Natalie Czech, as well as Ashley Hrycyshyn, of Bruja Collective, for providing the cover art and lots of the lettering art herein. Natalie was also my consistent soundboard throughout the writing of the book and has been an emotional supporter long before that. Her patience with my antics and outbursts is nothing shy of heroic.

To Max Green, though I'm not exactly sure what he does, I know without him I wouldn't have had enough time to sit down and complete this project. He manned the helm at "the little bar that could" so that I'd have the opportunity to shine. Surely, the light will beam on him next. And to Todd Bryant, for never missing an opportunity to help me with the research necessary to make this book happen.

To Robert O. Simonson for being a good steward of information and sharing it with the world through his books as well as his writings in The Gray Lady.

To Dale DeGroff, Gaz Regan, Erick Castro, Ryan Maybee, Jamie Boudreau, franky marshall, Nick Bennett, Derek Brown, Sarah Morrissey and Rick Dobbs for being willing to share a drink and a story with me. I hope I've made you proud to be a part of this. And to David Wondrich, Amanda Schuster, Jeffrey Morgenthaler, Maggie Hoffman, Jim Meehan and Kara Newman, I thank for the well wishes and kind words. You're all legends in my field, and I'm humbled to have your praise.

I also want to thank all of the women and men who've tended to me over their bars. Without the opportunity to sit and talk with them while observing their works, I'd never have amassed enough information to fill more than a matchbook. I wish them all a good and prosperous shift. And thank you, for reading.

Finally, even though it kept autocorrecting "branca" to "brands," I'd like to thank my iPhone 7, which I used to write this entire book. You're in my personal cell phone hall of fame.

There is only one reward for hard work and that's more work. So, I'll be getting back to it now.

ERIC MEDSKER

It's amazing to work on a project where my creative approach is trusted as fully as it was on this one. I was given the freedom to play, without inhibitions, in the medium I love. It's been an incredibly creative and fulfilling experience, and for that I must thank Sother Teague, for being such an exceptional collaborator, Jeff Ashworth, for bringing this whole crazy project together with humor and grace, and Catherine Armanasco, for originally championing my work and for keeping the rest of us degenerates on track. I'd also like to thank my collaborator in life, the Bonnie to my Clyde, Abigail Baldwin-Medsker: Your love and support is beyond measure.

JEFF ASHWORTH

Thanks of course to Sother for having enough faith in me to think that a guy he once had to teach how to make a Sazerac mid-shift would be the right person to bring his first book (there will be more) to life. Many thanks to Eric, who as Sother has already pointed out, was an absolute blast to work with and a true professional in every sense of the word (even when his equipment was inadvertently held hostage for 48 hours). Humblest of thanks to the entire team at Media Lab Books, without whom this title would only exist as a series of text messages and emails between Sother and myself—their names are on the masthead but they deserve to be on billboards. And to my wife, Lindsey, for recognizing I'm not lying when I say I have to drink for work, and for having the good sense to keep me honest about it anyway, particularly when I'm working too hard.

Media Lab Books
For inquiries, call 646-838-6637

Copyright 2018 by Sother Teague

Published by Topix Media Lab
14 Wall Street, Suite 4B
New York, NY 10005

Printed in China

ISBN-13: 978-0-9987898-4-2
ISBN-10: 0-9987898-4-4

Indexing by R studio T, NYC

Cover by Bruja Collective. Endpapers and quote typography by Bruja Collective.

Additional Photography From: Alamy: p28 Hemis; p32 United Archives GmbH; p64 B. Christopher; p118 Age Fotostock; p121 Rolf Hicker Photography. Getty Images: p67 Margaret Bourke-White; p148 Bloomberg. Shutterstock: p17, 146. Courtesy The Metropolitan Museum of Art: p27. Courtesy EpicStyle.com: p129. Guest Bartender Photos: p38 Eric Medsker; p83 J.Ferrara Photography Inc/Courtesy Gaz Regan; p95 Brandon Cummins/Courtesy Ryan Maybee; p105 Gabe Fonseca/Courtesy Erick Castro; p129 Andrew Fawcett/Courtsey Jamie Boudreau; p139 Farrah Skeiky/Courtesy Derek Brown; p167 Lauren Coleman/Courtesy Rick Dobbs; p225 Courtesy Sarah Morrissey; p231 Jesse Hsu/Courtesy Nick Bennett; p240 Andrew Kist/Courtesy ms. franky marshall.

MORE PRAISE
FOR SOTHER TEAGUE

"Sother Teague is one of our country's greatest cocktail and spirits experts, and he has always shared his knowledge generously. Whether he's behind the stick at Amor y Amargo or the mic on *The Speakeasy*, he always has a tale to tell and an interesting sip to offer. I'm thrilled that we all get to spend more time with him in the pages of this book."

—MAGGIE HOFFMAN
author of *The One-Bottle Cocktail: More than 80 Recipes with Fresh Ingredients and a Single Spirit*

"There are few people in the world with Sother's experience and knowledge when it comes to all things bitter. I was fortunate enough to spend an hour behind his bar once, and it was a lesson I won't soon forget."

—JEFFREY MORGENTHALER
author of *The Bar Book: Elements of Cocktail Technique and Drinking Distilled: A User's Manual*

"Sother Teague is kind of like the iPhone of bartenders—you don't know how much you need him in your life until you meet him for the first time. If he writes as well as his sense of hospitality and loyalty, we're all in for a good read. May he have everlasting battery life."

—AMANDA SCHUSTER
author of *New York Cocktails* and editor in chief of AlcoholProfessor.com

"To say that Sother Teague is a bitter man would be an understatement, but the world would be a bitter place if this Man a L'amari never achieved the impossible dream and created a book that allowed the world to experience his manic genius in the best of conditions: in the comfort of our homes with all doors double-locked, and Mr. Teague several leagues removed from our refuge."

—JAMIE BOUDREAU
author of *The Canon Cocktail Book: Recipes from the Award-Winning Bar*

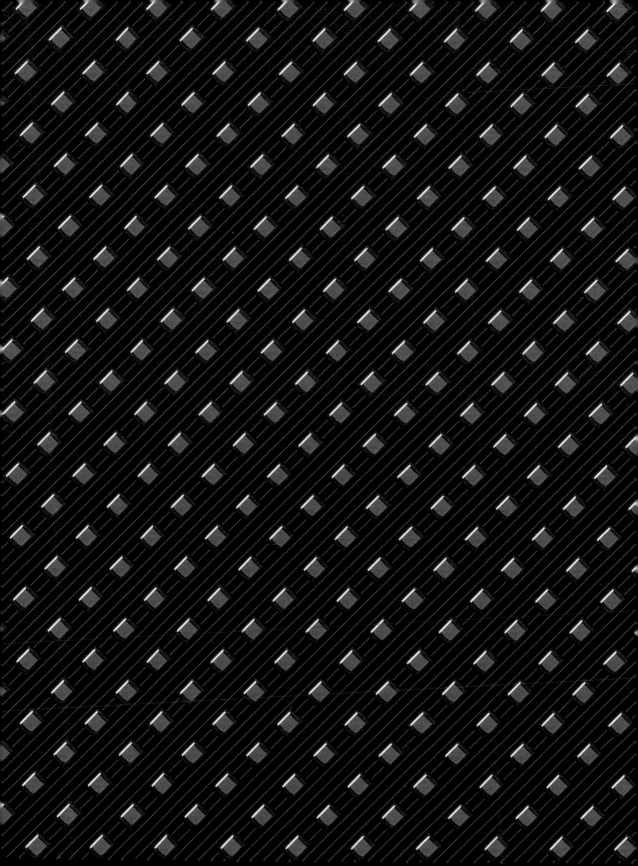